ASHES TO GOLD

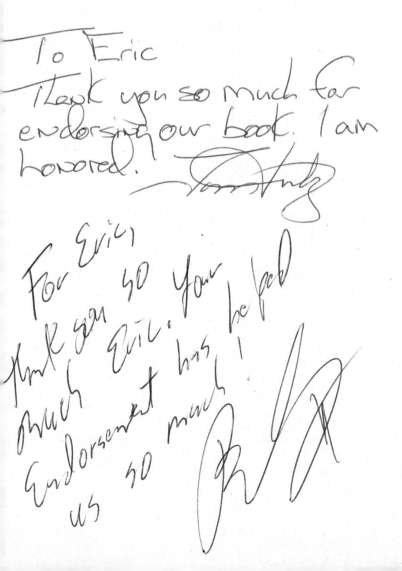

To Eric
Thank you so much for
endorsing our book. I am
honored.

For Eric,
thank you so
much Eric. Your
Endorsement has helped
us so much!

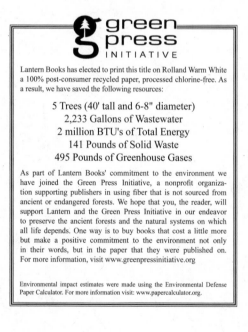

ASHES
to GOLD

The Alchemy of Mentoring
the Delinquent Boy

Brad Fern, MA, LAMFT
and Tom Lutz, MA, LP, LICSW

LANTERN BOOKS • NEW YORK • A DIVISION OF BOOKLIGHT INC.

2011
Lantern Books
128 Second Place
Brooklyn, NY 11231
www.lanternbooks.com

Printed in the United States of America

Print ISBN: 9781590563069
Ebook ISBN: 9781590563076

Library of Congress Cataloging-in-Publication Data
Fern, Brad.
 Ashes to gold : the alchemy of mentoring the
delinquent boy / Brad Fern and Tom Lutz.
      p. cm.
 Includes bibliographical references.
 ISBN 978-1-59056-306-9 (alk. paper) —
ISBN 978-1-59056-307-6
 1. Male juvenile delinquents—Counseling of.
 2. Male juvenile delinquents—Rehabilitation.
 3. Behavior disorders in adolescence.
I. Lutz, Tom. II. Title.
 HV9069.F385 2011
 364.36—dc22
                          2011017217

Contents

Acknowledgments

FOR DECADES, AT CONFERENCES ALL ACROSS THE UNITED States, the writer Robert Bly has challenged many minds and set many young hearts on fire. His poetry and prose have been translated into many languages around the globe, confirming him as one of the great literary minds of the late twentieth century. The authors of this book have been greatly influenced by his passion and his intellect. His advice and guidance regarding the meaning of images and archetypes in this book have been invaluable.

Our ability to walk in the world as community-minded men, our capacity to love and honor the women in our lives, and our competence as fathers are directly proportional to our friendships with quality men. Thanks to the Minneapolis Sufi Singing Group and the Saturday Men's Circle. Thanks to Jeff Davies for his generous support, and to Rick Larson and Troy Friedges for teaching the meaning of friendship. Thanks to Mike Shimek and Greg Heberlein for decades of partnership on the path.

Thanks also:

To John Lutz and William Lutz, who are now men; to Cici and Max Fern for "many little wild wishes"; to our wives and best friends, Karen Ward and Kelly Fern, for their love and support during the writing process; to Scott Edelstein for his advice about writing and publishing in general; to Patty Nieman for her editing skill; to Bob Roberts of Project Return in New Orleans for walking the soul-man walk; to the teacher who chooses to work anonymously in Minnesota, and whose ideas informed many of the thoughts in this book.

Most of all, special thanks to the boys whose stories appear *Ashes to Gold*. All the examples in this book are based on real events that have happened to young people. Identifying information in the case histories discussed has been omitted to the extent this has been possible. We admire these young men for their perseverance through often unspeakable adversity.

Finally, a word about voice. Unless specified, the "I" belongs to Brad.

Midway life's journey I was made aware

That I had strayed into a dark forest,

And the right path appeared not anywhere.

Ah, tongue cannot describe how it oppressed,

This wood, so harsh, dismal and wild, that fear

At thought of it strikes now into my breast.

From *The Divine Comedy*[1]
Inferno, Canto I
by Dante Alighieri
Translation, Laurence Binyon

Introduction

Myth, Mentoring, and a Steep Learning Curve

UP TO THE DAY I BEGAN AN INTERNSHIP AT AN URBAN Minnesota adolescent correctional-treatment facility, I thought of adolescents, especially delinquent adolescent males, as gangly, wild, and rude creatures. They were the ones who disrupted movies and acted crazy at the mall. I figured that after a couple of months I'd complete the internship and be off to counsel the more grounded and mature members of society.

To my surprise, after meeting only a few sets of angry, wounded eyes, I was hooked. I couldn't believe the stories I was hearing about violence and neglect, alcoholism and drug abuse, and more. I was astonished at the overwhelming level of cruelty and dysfunction most of these young men had endured. I soon realized that incarcerated boys are very easy to love, and it didn't take long to realize that not one of the troubled personalities I met had been born that way. They had all been made. If their parents hadn't wounded them, their peers had; and if neither peers nor parents were responsible, then it was the crime and chaos surrounding these boys that had bent their young spines.

Under layers of defensiveness and machismo, each boy had a painful story to tell—harrowing accounts of heartache, sorrow, and courage. I met boys and young men whom I came to admire. I witnessed scores of young lives at their crossroads, choosing which path to travel. Some were veering toward prison, death, destruction, and other nihilistic expressions of discouragement. Others, however, thanks to the hard work of many dedicated individuals, were leaning toward the road of responsibility, stability, and maturity.

I'd been assigned to the sixteen- to nineteen-year-old boys in the facility, and instructed to choose six or seven workable individuals. There were about twenty boys in my section, and they were an intimidating lot. Many were tattooed and unkempt. Some were much bigger than I was. I walked in the first day all touchy-feely, smiling, and set to be a do-gooder. Most of the boys either ignored me or sneered. I'd fallen face-first at the foot of a very, very, steep learning curve.

Because I was an apprentice, one of my responsibilities was to meet with the head psychologist, Tom Lutz, once a week for hour-long mentoring sessions. In the beginning, the sessions comprised straightforward progress reports summarizing how the boys had acted, what the boys had said, and how I had responded. Although Lutz encouraged the fruitful things I'd done, he also hatcheted my blundering and squashed my naiveté. I'd grown up in the milquetoast, white suburbs of Minneapolis where "Minnesota nice" reigned and the worst crisis my neighborhood ever experienced was Dutch elm disease. It seemed that all I had to offer was a glimpse into my idealism and my humanity—a world that was foreign to the boys. It wasn't long before several of the more crafty ones had me spun around and standing on my head. For the sincere boys, however, the ones who could admit they were wounded and floundering, I seemed to be of some use.

My gradual ascension on the learning curve eventually freed Lutz to talk less about my dearth of counseling skills and more about his treatment methods. I became fascinated with his therapeutic philosophy regarding delinquent teens. Instead of rote instruction for the boys, Lutz used allegorical stories. He had steeped himself in the mythopoetic/Jungian teachings of Robert Bly, Michael Meade, James Hillman, and others. Mythologies, fairy tales, and poems, Lutz believed, externalized pathology so angry boys were less likely to get defensive. The stories implanted templates in their young heads, something they could carry with them and look back on, long into their adult spiritual and emotional journeys.

The first time I tried using a story in a session, I was

amazed at its impact. I used an image from the *Odyssey* in a session with a young man I'll call Derek. Derek had been doing very well in the program. His attitude was exemplary. He had followed the rules, and he had shown great progress in his chemical-dependency treatment program. As a result, the staff had rewarded him with a weekend home furlough, which he went on and returned from without incident. Derek reported, however, that his girlfriend had visited him while he was at home. They were hugging and kissing and doing some of the things young lovers do together, and she reportedly suggested that he forget about returning to the facility. The two of them could cuddle, she said, along with some even more exciting activities. He related how hard it had been to trade her soft, feminine beauty and wonderful smell for the dank sterility of cinder block walls and bunks.

"Derek, do you know about Odysseus?" I asked.

Derek shook his head, no.

"Odysseus," I continued, "was a Greek hero from a long time ago. Once, the story goes, a wise old woman warned him about something called a siren. A siren is a mythical sea creature that sings a song—a melody that drives sailors crazy. It causes them to forget where they're going, so they run their ships onto the rocks and they drown.

"After years of being away from home, Odysseus was traveling back to his wife and son. He had no choice but to pass within earshot of the sirens. Do you know what he did to get past the sound of their song?"

Derek shook his head again.

"Odysseus instructed his men to stuff their ears with beeswax and then tie him to the mast of the ship. He told them on no account to let him go, even if he begged them. Sure enough, Odysseus was able to hear the siren song, and he pleaded with his crew, but they did not untie him. As a result, the ship was not smashed on the rocks and he was able to make it home. Get it?"

Derek's brow wrinkled with a hint of confusion.

"There will be many times when you will have to stuff wax into your ears," I continued, "or you will need the help of someone who has. I'm not saying this girl is bad, Derek. Maybe she will be your wife like Odysseus' wife, and she'll be the one you go home to. I'm saying that you have to get good at ignoring other people's bad ideas. It sucks being here, but part of your voyage home is to complete the program. It was extremely good that you stuffed wax in your ears and didn't listen to her. Your ship is still sailing. Get it?"

Derek smiled and nodded enthusiastically.[2]

After several weeks during which Lutz and I discussed stories we could tell the boys, we suddenly realized that

we had no story for our own use. We had no mythological template to guide us on our path as therapists working with adolescent males. We realized that we needed a
story that could illuminate our path like the *Odyssey* had
illuminated Derek's.

Finding the right story was no easy task. We needed a
mythical *mentor* (the word itself comes from the name
of an older friend of Odysseus) who imposed himself on
an apprentice for the apprentice's own good. In many
of the old stories, the young heroes seek out the mentor. They are proactive, often pursuing a goal of some
sort. They make profound mistakes along their journeys,
but they persevere until some external force helps them
toward a productive end.

Delinquent males are different. Far from proactively
searching for mentorship, they tend to run from guidance. They shun, for instance, the Herculean task of
sitting through the hundreds of lectures necessary to
graduate from high school, or they lack the humility to
learn a trade.

Therefore, in our search for a story to guide us, we
concluded that Hercules, Theseus, Lancelot, or any
other proactive hero would be of no use to us. We
needed a proactive-mentor story, one in which an elder
seeks out the young man—a young man who is lost and
maybe even a bit resistant. Our search went on and on

for months—books, libraries, friends—but no luck. Suddenly, fate turned our way.

Psychologist Jere Truer (who is also a musician and storyteller) heard about our quest and suggested we consult the Brothers Grimm. "There is a fairy tale," he said, "in which an old man approaches a young, lost lad, offering instruction and initiation." The name of that tale is "The Devil's Sooty Brother."

We immediately dove into the story and discovered its wealth of images. Because neither of us is a mythologist, we consulted the masters of mythology to teach us. We turned to Marie-Louise von Franz, the brilliant Jungian psychologist who turned Antoine de Saint-Exupéry's *The Little Prince* into a vehicle for unmasking the immature forever-boy, *Puer Aeternus*. We turned to Joseph Campbell for his staggering wealth of mythological analysis and interpretation. And most of all, we turned to Robert Bly for his work on the Grimm Brothers' fairy tale "Iron Hans" in his book *Iron John*. The outline for our book relies heavily on Bly's work. Bly has also written and lectured extensively about "The Devil's Sooty Brother," and he was kind enough to advise us.

This book discusses the story in some detail. It explores some of the central themes of the life passages of a teenage boy and provides many examples from the lives of those we've met—both "soldiers" and "Dark

Men"—who've worked through this challenging but vital period in a young man's life. We believe that *From Ashes into Gold* will prove useful for anyone who has struggled with an angry teenage boy, and especially for parents of troubled teen boys, teachers, and treatment and corrections professionals.

—B. F.

One

The Boy Steps Out

Metaphor: from the Greek pherein, meaning "to carry," and meta, meaning "beyond."

ALL PERCEPTION IS SYMBOLIC. EVENTS LIVE IN FLASH images in our memories, like frames from old motion pictures. We collect moments in time and space via our senses and then pass them through our filters of perception, interpretation, opinion, recall, and so on. We then turn events into mental iconography. Because humans are social animals, we often rely on collective metaphors to assign meaning to these icons. In other words, we depend on narratives, stories, myths, and legends to make sense of the world around us.

The heroes of these stories are metaphoric guides. They are often bumbling and inept, yet they strive, in spite of themselves, to shape their lives and their respective destinies. The Arthurian hero Parzival, for example, is sheltered by his mother as a boy and is a tragic buffoon as a young man. He embodies the consequences of naïve ambition and narcissism. It is through his transitional acts of honesty, chivalry, and bravery that he eventually becomes the keeper of the Holy Grail.[3]

Other mythological heroes are blessed with competency from the start. Beowulf is distinguished in his formative years by his physical strength. He meets his destiny head on by saving a whole settlement, slaying the man-eating half-monster Grendel, and then killing Grendel's hideous monster mother. There are countless stories like these—stories of boys actively transforming themselves into men.

In "The Devil's Sooty Brother," a reluctant young hero requires an elder to turn him or trick him, in much the same way delinquent boys need to be tricked or forced to turn toward community-mindedness. Though the Brothers Grimm, Jacob and Wilhelm, recorded "The Devil's Sooty Brother" sometime in the early nineteenth century, Robert Bly reminds us that this story could be thousands of years old.[4]

The Devil's Sooty Brother[5]

A young man, a corporal, who had been recently discharged from the military, entered a forest and eventually found himself lost and hungry. After a time wandering around in the woods, he ran into a little, dark man, whom the lad believed to be the devil.

"What is wrong with you, young man?" the Dark Man inquired. "You look so sad."

"I am lost and hungry, and I have no money," said the corporal, with a quality of longing in his voice.

"Well, if you work for me and do a good job, then you will have everything you could ever need. Serve me for seven years and then you shall be paid, but during those seven years you cannot bathe, comb your hair, cut your fingernails, or wipe the tears from your eyes."

The young man decided that dealing with the devil was better than starving or freezing to death. Since he was desperate, he agreed to the Dark Man's terms. The Dark Man led the corporal deep beneath the ground to a fiery realm. The corporal saw pots boiling upon the fires.

"For seven years you must keep the fires stoked and the pots boiling. But there is one thing that you must not do," said the Dark Man to the lad. "Under no circumstances can you look into the pots."

The Dark Man returned to the earth to do his work and left the corporal to do his. After a time, the boy's curiosity got the better of him. He looked into one of the pots and saw his former lieutenant.

"You had power over me," the young man taunted, "and now I have power over you."

He then slammed the lid shut and stoked the fire to increase the discomfort of his former superior. Likewise, the young man looked into a second pot. He saw his colonel and taunted him as well.

"You once had power over me, and now I have power over you." And, once again, he slammed the lid shut and stoked up the fire.

He looked into a third pot and inside was his general.

Again, "You once had power over me, and now I have power over you." The corporal slammed the lid shut and turned up the heat.

The Dark Man returned and saw immediately that the boy had disobeyed his orders.

"You are lucky that you stoked the fires under the pots after looking into them. If you had not, you would have died," said the little man. "You have defied me." The Dark Man took all the ashes that the lad had swept up and put them in a bag. "This is your pay. Now, do you want to go back home?"

"Yes," said the boy. "I'd like to see how my father is doing."

"Then take this bag of sweepings and go. But if anyone asks where you are coming from you must say 'Hell.'

If anyone asks who you are, say, 'I'm the devil's sooty brother and my king as well.'"

The lad was not happy with what he had been given, but he kept quiet and followed the Dark Man's instructions. He emerged from hell and was delighted to discover that the sweepings had turned to gold. He entered the city and soon came by an inn. The innkeeper saw the lad and was terrified.

"Where are you coming from?" the innkeeper called.

"Hell," the boy replied.

"And who are you?"

"I am the devil's sooty brother and my king as well."

The innkeeper balked at the lad's appearance: his hair was tangled, his nails were long, and tear tracks could be seen through the soot on his face. The innkeeper thought about ways to turn the young man away. But as the young man came nearer, the innkeeper saw the gold and showed him in.

The young man insisted on the best room and the finest service. He did not bathe or groom himself, in accordance with the Dark Man's instructions, but he ate and drank his fill.

In the middle of the night, the innkeeper couldn't get the young man's riches out of his mind. He snuck into the corporal's room and stole the gold.

When the corporal discovered that the innkeeper had stolen his gold, he pulled himself together but wasted little time ruminating. "Your luck has gone bad," he said to himself, "but through no fault of your own." He went back to the Dark Man, told him what had happened, and asked for help.

"Sit down," the Dark Man said. He then cut the young man's hair and nails, bathed him, and wiped the tears from his eyes. "Now you go back to the innkeeper," he said, "and tell him to return the money to you. Say to him that if he refuses he will have to come down here and tend the fires like you did, and he will have to look as bad, too."

The boy did as the Dark Man said, and the landlord gave the money back plus interest. The corporal was now rich.

The young man set his mind back to finding his father. He bought a smock and played music, a skill he had learned while tending the pots. The local king heard him playing music and fell in love with what he was hearing. "Play for me," the king said, "and I will wed you to my daughter."

But when the king's oldest daughter found out that her betrothed wore a smock, she threatened to drown herself. The king's youngest daughter, however—who could recognize a quality young man when she saw one—married the corporal on the spot. When the king died, the corporal and his bride inherited the whole realm.

Devil or Healer?

Since the inception of religious thought, one culture's sacred spirit has been another's devil. Remnants of that sort of spiritual competition are evident throughout the United States. The Native Americans sanctified particular lakes, rivers, and geographic areas. But when the European settlers took over, they denigrated these sacred landmarks because they feared the native deities and considered them to be evil. In Wisconsin, for instance, Manidoo Gamii (Spirit Lake) became Devil's Lake.

The Brothers Grimm were Calvinists, and almost certainly it was they—or the people relating the stories to them—who introduced the satanic reference to the pre-Christian "devil" character in this story. This qualification is important, for there is an ocean of difference between the Dark Man in this story and the Biblical Satan.

Notice, for example, that the Grimms' character is actually a healer. We commonly think of healers as transforming us from sickness to health. We recognize doctors as healers, for instance, but there are other, less obvious forms of healing. Hospice workers help terminal patients pass through death with dignity and emotional continuity. A healer then, in a deeper sense, is one who helps someone change—often through crisis. Priests, rabbis, and imams deal with spiritual transformation. They are all healers.

In "The Devil's Sooty Brother," the young man is in the midst of a crisis of transformation—he is becoming a man. The Dark Man helps him change and is, therefore, a healer. The methods of the Dark Man are shamanic in nature. Archetypically, he is associated with the magician or the alchemist. He is dark like the Hindu goddess Kali ("The Black One") who is likewise associated with change. The biblical Satan, conversely, would not have aided a young traveler's transformation. He would have worked to keep him immature and controllable. He would have kept him a dependant, chronic forever-boy.

Instead, the Dark Man displays genuine compassion for the young man. He begins by noticing the corporal's pain: "What's wrong with you, young man? You look so sad." It is true that the Dark Man does not protect the boy from pain, but that is because he is not trying to control him. Furthermore, the lad's going down beneath the ground is an initiatory act and for his own good. If the Dark Man were Satan, he would use false compassion to seduce our hero, and our corporal would end up trapped somehow.

In his discussion of this story, Robert Bly offers "Dark Man" as a more neutral and appropriate alternative to the appellation "devil." The authors of this book agree, so henceforth the words "Dark Man" will replace the word "devil," and the words "beneath the earth" will replace the word "hell."

Narcissism, the Community, and Hyper-Structure

All boys, delinquent or not, emerge from childhood not ready to be responsible community members. They must be wrested from infantile narcissism or guided through the conflicted state of adolescent self-absorption.

Infants, especially until the age of around three, are narcissistic by design. From a developmental perspective, this biological requirement is easy to understand. The child instinctively demands to be fed, cleaned, and protected: "I don't care that it's four in the morning. Get in here now, wipe my bottom, and feed me. I need to eat every couple of hours, and I don't care how tired it makes you!" This is the age-appropriate claim made by all infants.

Until the third month, babies are confused about their separation from the mother's womb. It's not unusual to see babies surprised by their own hands passing in front of their eyes. They hold their fingers up to their faces in wonderment, flexing and moving the digits around to study their contours and functions.

The mere presence of the mother's body comforts the child. Against the mother's bosom, the child smells the familiar aroma, feels the beat of her heart, and hears the sound of her voice. Around and after the third month, the child begins to realize that the mother is actually a separate entity.

Until the eighteenth month, the child still emphasizes the maternal connection and perceives the father as an interesting, reassuring, and amusing curiosity. The child's world is very small and still revolves around getting his or her needs met. It isn't until the third year, if conditions are right, that children begin to break free of infantile narcissism. It is the job of both parents to help the child make that break, and transform a self-centered toddler into a young person with manners, self-control, and a concern for the welfare of others in the family.

A second wave of narcissism hits around the time of adolescence, but this second wave is inappropriate and must not be indulged by the parent. Adolescent narcissism must be transformed into community-mindedness. And parents cannot facilitate this process alone. Teachers, counselors, coaches, and other adults must join in to enable the change. To produce a community man, the community must participate. The qualities that must replace narcissism in the adolescent are concern for the community at large and an ability to understand the conceptual needs (rules, laws, etc.) of that community. Of course, this is easier said than accomplished.

When we think of the military, we think of order. We picture in our minds a meritocracy and a paternalistic hierarchy. The parental structures that contain children are similar to military ones. In the story, our corporal has been discharged from the army. He has stepped out of the necessary rule-immersed existence that is childhood—as all young men must. He has emerged from parental control but, like many others, finds himself lost without it.

Delinquent adolescent males are walking contradictions. Down to their bones, their energy is often topsy-turvy, and they tend to reject hierarchy. Steve Hirschorn has written: "Of all mistaken goals [attention, power, revenge, or avoidance] delinquents seem most likely to aspire to power. Their sense of belonging is achieved by resisting adults."[6] Delinquents rightly expect to separate from the old filial boundaries and limitations, but they lack the emotional and psychic girth necessary to bear adult responsibility. This predicament pits a violent abhorrence of structure against a tremendous need for it.

Correctional treatment programs depressurize delinquents by removing them from chaos and immersing them back in structure—a military-style, community-imposed hyper-structure. Hyper-structure, in this way, becomes a re-parenting mechanism rather than a punishment or simply an antidote for the chaos the young men have experienced.

There is an old Korean adage about quality men: *He is one who doesn't need laws.* The paramount indicator of a delinquent's ability to change is the emergence of an essential component of maturity—the recognition of the need for rules and laws—which, paradoxically, renders the rules unnecessary. Once this quality begins to appear, the corrections structure is slowly relaxed.

The Descent

There is a difference between knowing and understanding. Knowing is a mental construct, while true understanding involves emotion. Empathy, sympathy, fear, appropriate anger, sadness—all are necessary components of true understanding. Intellectual realizations alone do not turn a delinquent from a destructive path. He must also generate an emotional change if recovery is going to be meaningful and to last. Of course, facilitating emotional change is more difficult than facilitating cerebral insights. That is why so many delinquents end up dead. They might be able to say that their lives are a mess, but they refuse to turn downward and grieve that cruel actuality.

The Dark Man in the story requires the boy to go down into a fiery underworld and the boy agrees. This kind of downward motion, along with the young corporal's grimy appearance, signify his willingness to experience grief, to walk in the unsightly and foul state of sorrow. When someone truly grieves, they don't look good. The Dark Man then prohibits the corporal from combing his hair, cutting his nails, and bathing. He doesn't allow the boy to wipe the tears from his eyes, requiring the boy to own his grief.

It has been said that wounded people wound people. The wounds sustained by children, especially boys, cause them to lash out when they get older, worsening those wounds and accentuating their own pain, *ad infinitum*. It's much like a snowball rolling down a hill, getting bigger and gaining momentum as it goes. Angry young men often find themselves caught in a cycle that is destructive both to themselves and their community, simply because they won't stop to feel and release the grief that they carry. We see examples of that grief later on in this book.

Emotional and psychic wounds essentially allow two alternatives to anyone who has been wounded. The first is to go down into grief willingly. Like the mystics, we can welcome or even celebrate our grief. Since wounds are inevitable and grief is the essential healing balm, this first alternative is the wiser. The second alternative is not really a choice. Instead of accepting or welcoming grief, grief can reach up and drag us down. Many of the *Diagnostic and Statistical Manual of Mental Disorders'* Axis 1 disorders can be traced to unexpressed grief: sleep problems, eating disorders, sexual dysfunction, and depression, to name only a few. Boys who resist grieving are likewise pulled down by depression, addiction, and wounded egos. And it often kills them.

Early in "The Devil's Sooty Brother," the Dark Man requires the boy neither to comb his hair, bathe, nor wipe the tears from his eyes. These prohibitions, as we have said, are metaphors for instructing the young man to accept and express grief. But the prohibition about not looking into the pots is different. By forbidding the boy to look into the pots, the Dark Man is enticing the boy, using a kind of curiosity jujitsu. The moment the boy is told not to look, the reader knows exactly what he will do. He *will* look into the pots because an elder has told him not to.

Minnesota poet Timothy Young, who has worked extensively with delinquent teens, says there is no better way to get a teenage boy to do what you want than by telling him not to do it. Practically speaking, when a family-system issue presents itself, the therapist might say, for example, "You don't have to look at this issue if you don't want to." The therapist essentially points and says, "You don't have to go over there and peek into that pot. Really, your mother's crack-cocaine dealing wasn't a problem? Having all those gangsters coming around all the time wasn't a problem for you and your siblings? Was it?"

In the Garden of Eden myth, God entices Adam in a similar way. Adam was forbidden to leave his innocence behind, forbidden to become conscious, to taste the fruit of knowledge: "She took of its fruit and ate, and she also gave some to her husband who was with her, and he ate. Then the eyes of both were opened, and they knew that they were naked" (Genesis 3:6, ESV). Adam chose to live as an adult man by entering communion with a woman and shouldering the resultant consciousness. This effectively banished Adam from filial bliss, the naiveté of childhood in which the lions sleep with the lambs. Eating the fruit banished him to a conscious life that carries the burden of conscious choice.[7]

Our corporal, then, assumes the burden of consciousness by looking into the pots. But what do the pots represent?

The Pots

When we imagine the Dark Man's underground workplace, we may picture a cave-like space in the earth, containing many large cauldrons set upon fires with smoke and ash all around. Our corporal labors intensely, shoveling coal and hefting wood to keep the pots cooking. He has descended into the deep emotional world to complete a task, but it is he who is actually being transformed, through hard psychic and emotional work. It is he who is actually being cooked. And he is being cooked by the Dark Man.

In a famous poem by the thirteenth-century Sufi poet Jalaluddin Rumi, a cook knocks a chickpea back into a boiling pot. The chickpea begs, "Why are you doing this to me?" The cook answers:

> You think I'm torturing you.
> I'm giving you flavor,
> so you can mix with spices and rice
> and be the lovely vitality of a human being.[8]

In addition to the writings of the Grimm Brothers and Rumi, other instances of cooking as a metaphor for psychic, emotional, and spiritual transformation exist. The idea of a cauldron as a magical cooking vessel is found in the collection of Welsh mythological tales called the *Mabinogion*. One of those tales, "Branwen, Daughter of Llyr," tells of a mythical titan named Bran the Blessed who possesses a great pot in which dead soldiers are

cooked overnight until they come back to life.[9] The Holy
Grail is believed by some to be a form of this cauldron.[10]

Afagddu is another Mabinogian character. He is the
ugliest man in the world and son of the hag-goddess
Ceridwen. To appease Afagddu for his horrible looks,
Ceridwen creates a cauldron and orders an old man and
a young boy (Gwion) to tend it. Some of the hot liquid
splashes on Gwion's fingers as he stirs the pot, and he
instinctively licks them to ease the pain, thus ingesting
some of the liquid. He is then gifted with the compensa-
tion that was meant for Ceridwen's ugly son, the gift of
great knowledge. Ceridwen then chases Gwion until she
finally swallows him, births him, sews him into a seal-
skin, and throws him into the ocean.[11]

The images in these stories rely heavily on ancient
Celtic mythology. Since various Celtic tribes occupied
the land spanning from modern day Spain to Turkey, and
since the epicenter of ancient Celtic culture has been
placed in modern-day southern Germany,[12] it is quite
possible that the Bavarian Grimm Brothers' stories were
influenced by Celtic mythology as well. Therefore, it
is reasonable to see the Dark Man's pots as life-giving,
transforming vessels.

Furthermore, the underworld of ancient Welsh mythology (Annwn) was imagined as a place that mortals
could visit in order to tap ancestral forces.[13] Unlike the

Christian version of the underworld, a place where sinners are sent to be punished, the Dark Man's subterranean workplace is a supernatural, ancestral axis.

But why, with a whole universe of personalities and symbols, are there three military officers in the pots? It is quite possible that the story itself sprung from resentment of abusive military leaders over the centuries. Our corporal has been released from the military and may have an ax to grind. Europe throughout the ages has had no shortage of wars and abused soldiers. Bly, however, insists that it is essential for readers to keep the image of cooking in the realm of metaphor. There is no *human* general or *human* lieutenant whom this story is suggesting should be abused. He suggests that cooking in the Dark Man's cave corresponds to the interior quality of a young man, his ability to sit with things for a long time. The delayed gratification exemplified by going to college, learning a trade, or working with a psychotherapist for an extended period of time are all ways in which a young man can tend his cooking pots.

Minneapolis-based spiritual counselor Judith Pryor suggests that the officers in the pots represent the young man's suffering, which is being transformed into something productive. The ability to fight on the street (battlefield) becomes transformed into fighting for peace or justice, and the like.

The three military men in the pots may also represent the boy's internalized beliefs that once controlled him—mistaken notions, peer pressure, family issues, self-deceptions, etc. This interpretation is especially apropos when we think of young people liberated from membership in gangs. Three gang leaders, for instance, would be in the pots. "You told me that I would be beaten or shot if I ever left the gang," a recovering gang member might say. "Now I will turn my capacity for aggression against you, and I will stand up to you." Other commentators have suggested that the three superiors represent external forces: societal ills, crime, drugs, and alcohol abuse, etc.

Turning up the heat under the pots can also characterize raising the stakes within the family. A boy who has endured beatings at home might have concluded, "I believe that I am worthless right down to the soles of my feet. Why else would my father have beat me?" After opening his eyes and turning up the heat, he might say, "My father is an abusive drunkard," thereby placing the blame for the physical abuse where it actually belongs. He may say to his father, "Your beatings once controlled my thinking, but now I do."[14] With this shift, the son puts the heat on the father instead of himself, and if the boy wants to heal emotionally and psychically, he'll turn it up.

Two

The Legacy of Our Fathers

IN 1985, OR THEREABOUTS, WE HEARD MICHAEL MEADE tell the following story at a men's conference:

> A father and son go out hunting together, and all they manage to kill is a rat. The father instructs his son to guard the carcass while he goes off to hunt other quarry. The son is embarrassed and despises the fact that all they have killed is a rat. He sees a graceful gazelle bounding through the grass nearby, and he runs after it. Of course, the gazelle easily outruns the boy. He returns to the spot where the rat had been, but another animal has taken it. The father returns empty-handed and is enraged that the boy did not guard the rat as he was instructed. The father strikes the boy, and they both go hungry that night.

This is a story about young men not being satisfied with the legacy they've inherited from their fathers. It warns against taking the father for granted, and warns against abandoning the father's influence for something ostentatious and unobtainable. But the story also warns against underestimating the impact of the father's legacy.

A delinquent boy may have never met his father, but he may still unknowingly walk his father's dysfunctional path. His mother or someone else in his life will see to it.

A father passes on more than just his genetic blueprint to the son. He also passes on his worldview, and this worldview affects career choice, romantic relationships, and emotional temperament. Treatment professionals can often describe a delinquent boy's father without ever meeting him. They simply look at the son and see the father through the young man's behavior. Many fathers of delinquent boys were delinquent boys themselves.

Michael, an incarcerated boy of seventeen, had a significant rage problem. He regularly blew up at peers and staff. The slightest provocation set him off. The staff at the facility could not figure out how to help Michael control his temper. Many interventions were attempted. All failed. Weeks later, Michael's father showed up at a family session, and the family dynamic became clear when the father stormed out after a relatively minor disagreement. The family then told the treatment professional that the father had a history of rage and acting it out inappropriately. Michael was just like his father.

Often, a delinquent boy will follow his father's path because it is dangerous not to. When the son of a delinquent man chooses to walk upright, he wounds both himself and his dysfunctional father. Choosing to walk a path that is different from the father's is like admitting that the father and the family are wrong or, more painfully, admitting that the father actually mattered.

That is why so many young men struggle when they discover that they must act differently than their fathers. Further complicating the issue, if delinquent boys stop their criminal ways, their mothers often get upset. Their siblings wonder who they are. Their friends disown them. When a delinquent boy refuses his emotional inheritance, he often has to abandon his family and friends and face the world alone. When one considers the staggering bind of this dilemma, it is not surprising that many delinquents do not change.

An important first step for redirecting a delinquent may be to make him conscious of the pain his father's behavior has caused him. Once again, we turn toward grieving.

Ashes Turned to Gold

Young gang members returning to their neighborhoods after treatment often begin to see how gang behavior has harmed their families and communities. They begin to de-sentimentalize some of their own relatives and begin to have compassion for, say, victims and cops. As "The Devil's Sooty Brother" recounts, these are the sweepings or ashes turning to gold, or painful work becoming something precious. The gold in this case is new emotional consciousness turned outward. The boys may still look unkempt despite the gold they have acquired—wild hair, sharp nails, and sooty tear tracks down their faces—but a tenuous connection has been established between past wounds and social awareness (the needs of others).

In Bly's *Iron John*, a boy runs away with a wild, hairy man, who places him near a magic stream and instructs him to keep out of the water. The lad, like our corporal and like Adam in the Garden of Eden, disobeys. His hair falls into the water and turns to gold. Rather than letting his gold show for all to see, however, this boy hides it beneath a scarf. He does so not because he is ashamed of it, but because he knows that it is valuable and worth protecting. The intrinsic wealth that he carries is eventually recognized by a girl. The boy's scarf falls off, exposing his golden locks to the sun, and the girl sees the reflection illuminating her bedroom wall. She recognizes the boy's value—as he has recognized his own value—and she tells her father.

The young man in *Iron John* knows humility and

demonstrates no desire to prostitute his gifts. The word "humility" is derived from the Latin *humus*, which means earth or ground. The protagonist in *Iron John* works as an apprentice to the king's gardener and humbly labors in the dirt with his head covered. This is opposite of, say, the mythological Greek flying boy, Icarus, whose wings disintegrate when his hubris brings him too close to the sun.

The corporal in "The Dark Man's Sooty Brother" parades into a strange town with his hard-earned gold hanging out for anyone to see. He stays in the best room the innkeeper has to offer, drinks the finest wine available, and eats to his fill. He forgets that he has come from the ground or under it. He momentarily loses his *humus*. This lapse is both natural and typical of young men who have been recently blessed by Dark Man wisdom. Bly warns that when you return from a journey to a sacred place, you must take care. People will try to steal what you've gained.

For instance, a boy might learn a useful therapeutic technique and tell his mother about it. His mother might say, "I know what you did with that counselor. We did that back in the eighties. Let's do that together." And the excitement of a new discovery is crushed. Or a father might act like the greedy innkeeper and use his son's progress to exonerate himself for past behavior: "Johnny's doing well now, evidence that my drinking has had little ill-effect upon him. The effect of my behavior really isn't that bad." This kind of parent, like a vampire, sucks the vibrant energy and excitement out of the recovering boy.

We often see vampire parents in treatment groups or family therapy. A son prepares for months to confront his father in the group for, say, physical abuse. The father says the right words. He's been in prison groups and Alcoholics Anonymous groups before. He knows the drill. He may apologize or even cry. The group members witness the feel-good moment and compliment the father. But the father does not, in fact, change. He keeps drinking, smoking pot, and abusing mom. And he effectively steals the boy's emotional energy. The father becomes a parasite to his son's emotional emergence, reducing the boy's emotional work to a mere look-good tool. We think of Goya's horrifying painting *Saturn Devouring His Son* when we see this kind of father. A Saturn-like father, a vampiric mother, the neighborhood gang, and the drug dealer are all exemplified by the greedy innkeeper.

Shame

In "The Devil's Sooty Brother," the corporal says to himself after the gold is stolen, "You have been unfortunate through no fault of your own!" It is a very good sign that the young man can do this. His psychic work is starting to pay off. He's not willing to waste time wallowing in shame. He doesn't retaliate to save face either, like so many angry delinquents do. Urban newspapers are filled with assaults and murders committed by young men who attack simply because they felt disrespected.

It is very important when a family or community steals the gold of a transformed young man that he not take on the blame, or get lost in shame. When a vampire bites you, you are at risk of becoming a vampire. Grief and consciousness are the garlic and wooden stake required to subdue this kind of vampire. In practice, the process often begins with denial first, then anger and sadness, and finally acceptance.

Additionally, an abandoned, neglected, or abused boy must realize that the pain he has endured is not his fault. Delinquent young men take little responsibility for things they should and, conversely, take too much responsibility for things that aren't their fault. (We will see a specific example of this later in the book.) For a delinquent teen to mature into a community-minded man, this paradox must be reversed. A recovering boy, when he goes back home, must know down to his bones that he is not his parents' behavior. He is not the gang mentality, nor the chaotic neighborhood he came from. He is separate, and he gets to choose.

An element of this need for self-mastery can be found in the enigmatic second half of the statement that the Dark Man tells the young man to say: "I'm the devil's sooty brother and my king as well." The emphasis here is on "my." The Dark Man is instructing the corporal to inform others that he is his own king. In other words, the young man has some mastery of his destiny, path, and ego. Or at least, that is what he should aspire to have. While they are only parroted words when first used, the young man will eventually grow into them and they will become his own. Eventually, the words will become a reality facilitated by good mentorship. The young man will, indeed, be his own king.

Ultimately, our corporal refuses the burden of shame. He accurately assigns the blame where it belongs— with the innkeeper. This signals individuation and ego strength. The corporal returns to the ancient wisdom of the Dark Man rather than raging or collapsing in shame at the loss of his gold. He refuses to feel shameful or let the desperate innkeeper make him desperate as well.

It might have seemed codependent or controlling when the Dark Man instructed the boy to return to the innkeeper and communicate a message from him. If the Dark Man truly wanted to empower the young man, why didn't he let him speak for himself?

We must keep in mind that when we're young almost

any profound thing we may say comes from other sources.[15] The deepest of our utterances may be regurgitated parts of lectures we've heard, passages of books we've read, or maybe a line from a poem. This is natural and it's better to admit it than to waste energy denying it. It is also nothing to denigrate. Before boys can speak with their own voices, they must speak with an elder's voice—a "valance," as one teacher put it. Place an obstacle in a young man's path and he is very likely to act as he has seen an older man or woman act.

The corporal returns to the Dark Man, marking the full transformation of his adolescent obstinacies into conscious humility. He now actively seeks mentoring. It's not because he is lost or hungry. The wisest teachers are perpetual students, and the young man is growing wise. The Dark Man grooms him, lends his voice, and sends him back.

Mack

Here is an example of a delinquent who transformed but failed to return to the Dark Man and paid the price. Eighteen-year-old Mack had managed, with the help of Tom Lutz, to go beneath the earth and turn up the emotional heat, but he emerged and lost his humility. He squandered his gold.

Mack's mother left his family when he was young and his parents divorced a few years later. His father, an alcoholic, was involved with gangs and was in and out of prison. Mack estimated that his father had beaten him thirty to forty times while he, Mack, had been between sixth and tenth grades. Instead of staying with his mother, who was mentally ill and addicted to crack cocaine, Mack often lived with extended family members, moving from town to town as he grew up. Nearly all of Mack's relatives openly used marijuana, crack, and other illicit drugs. When he was eleven, Mack witnessed his seventeen-year-old brother killed by the police.

Mack racked up a long history of assaults and robberies, and he had been involved with one of the local gangs. He was eventually placed in a corrections facility for several aggravated robberies, one using a forty-five caliber pistol.

Lutz noted that Mack had an average IQ and diagnosed him with Conduct Disorder, Adolescent Onset, Severe. Mack also suffered from anxiety; he was haunted by the feeling of being victimized by numerous staff and peers.

He was in the middle of a significant altercation when Lutz brought him in to talk.

"Why did you bring me here?" Mack asked. "I don't need to talk with you."

"It's true," Lutz replied, "you probably don't. You can continue to blow up, go back to court and have your sentence enforced and spend several years in prison, if you want. Or we can talk about what set you off?"

"Marko, the cook," Mack explained, "is always talking shit to me. He orders me around, and he's always disrespecting me. I'm tired of him, man."

"Okay, but you've blown up pretty consistently ever since you got here. I mean, if it's not the cook disrespecting you, it's one of the guys in the dorm. If it's not one of the guys in the dorm, it's the staff. The medication you take helps, but meds don't work alone. You have to put some effort into it."

"Fuck you."

"Okay, sure, but notice how well things are going with you trying to do it alone. You don't need to work with me, but you're smart enough to know that things are currently headed south."

After a moment of surly silence, Mack said, "Okay. Fine. I am tired of everybody kicking my ass."

"You know, it's possible that it's *you* who's no fun to be around."

"What do you mean?"

"Well, you're always snapping at people and consistently trying to prove that you are not to be messed with.

You maintain quite a shield. You know, other than Captain America, shields are generally used for defense."

A quizzical look replaced Mack's defensive expression.

"Shields are for fending off onslaughts of slings and arrows," Lutz continued. "I have this image of you, Mack, standing alone in the field with this big heavy iron shield and the enemy all around you. You know, like in those movies where the attackers let loose their arrows all at once and thousands of them come raining down. Well, there you are, alone, with only your shield, as you're being pelted by arrows like rain."

"Yeah, it's like that."

"Well, I have a few strategies that might be helpful, but we're out of time for now. Are you willing to learn them later?"

Mack nodded.

"Good. Let's talk at another time when we can get into this more thoroughly."

"Okay, thanks."

But Mack ran into trouble within the next twenty-four hours. Lutz was requested at one of the seclusion rooms, a bare room with a bunk, an observation window, and nothing with which an angry kid could hurt himself. He found Mack sitting on the bunk, looking dejected. Lutz wasted no time getting to the point.

"You know you suck at defending yourself," he said.

"What do you mean?"

"I mean if you were really good at defense, you wouldn't be in here."

"My primary [counselor/guard] put me in here," Mack said.

"No, it's that you *really* don't know how to defend yourself. Someone who was good at defending himself wouldn't get captured. You need some lessons."

Mack scowled.

"You don't know how to duck and move," Lutz continued. "You just stand there with your big ungainly shield, smashing it and your body around in an effort to defend yourself. You know that movie, *The Matrix*?"

"Yeah."

"Well, that scene where they're shooting at Neo and he dodges the bullets up on the roof. He ducks and moves. It is hard to catch him. You need to learn how to duck and move."

"Okay," Mack said with a tentative nod of his head.

"The first lesson is to know when danger is near before it has arrived. You wait too long. Our bodies tell us when danger is near. In fact, you've been around so much danger that you've developed an anxiety disorder. Your body actually is quite sensitive. Now that you're taking meds, you can get a more accurate read. Tell me where you feel anxious in your body."

Mack put his hand over his gut. "Well, I feel tight in my throat and in my stomach."

"Perfect. It's very simple. When you feel those feelings, you duck and then move away."

"What do you mean, duck?"

"You ignore the opposing army before they begin shooting. If you ignore them, then they don't perceive you to be a danger. You, on the other hand, wait until they're upon you and then you lift your shield, which begs them to shoot. It's like you're saying, 'Kick my ass.' So when you sense the warning signs, just leave the situation and settle down. Allow yourself to relax. Get away from people. Your warning signs are helpful to you. Listen to them."

"So, when I feel the warning signs, I should just go off and be by myself?"

"Exactly."

"What about staff? I just can't leave when it's the staff who are bugging me."

"Sure you can. Actually, we can set it up so that you can retreat to your bunk or a quiet place in the dorm for a while. However, you'll have to come back and finish things out."

"What do you mean?" Mack asked. "If I've ducked and moved, why should I do something else?"

"Well, now you're ready for my second thought. You've lived a life in which you perceive danger all the time, even from people who could be your allies. You need to learn who is really dangerous and who isn't. You need to shift perspectives. I want you to interview a number of the residents about who they trust, and then come back and let me know who is trustworthy and why. Meanwhile, we'll set it up for you to move away from danger."

"Yeah. Thanks, man."

Mack later reported feeling proud for avoiding two potential conflict situations, just by using this shift of perspective. He identified several staff and peers as trustworthy. He even began to get excited about recovery.

Mack continued with the one-on-one sessions for a few more weeks until he eventually appeared to have turned his behavior and his thinking around. He no longer perceived that others were always out to get him. Through the use of medications and the behavioral techniques taught to him by Lutz, he began to get his anger and anxiety under control. He did so well, in fact, that one-on-one sessions were eventually canceled.

Mack had a bright mind and the gift of charisma. One of his targeted job connections recognized his talent and hired him on the spot. Lutz and other staff arranged for Mack to be released for work, someone drove him to get a new pair of work boots. Another staff member drove him to get his cap and gown for graduation from the facility school.

Generally, Mack seemed to be doing well. Eventually, he was released from the facility, but then he ran into difficulties. He was having problems with a young woman whom he had met, and an enemy gang member called him and threatened him. It was the innkeeper after his gold.

Unfortunately, Mack returned to his tendency to go it alone. He began getting discouraged, but he didn't tell anyone about how he felt. He refused to go back under the ground. He didn't seek out the Dark Man. He went off of his medication. To avoid a possible confrontation with the gang member who phoned him, Mack began to miss work. Eventually, isolated and overwhelmed, he reverted to his father's example and was arrested for making terroristic threats. Mack is now facing prison time in the adult system. He emerged from beneath the ground with a bag of gold but refused to return to the Dark Man when it was stolen.

Fortunately, he is still young, and there will be more chances for him to turn. Lutz's good work was not in vain, for Mack may someday learn to accept that he will, like any other man, need mentorship throughout the course of his life.

Doran

Doran was five and a half feet tall and weighed all of one hundred fifty pounds. He was seventeen with a bright, inquisitive mind and fiery green eyes that leapt out from his boyish face. His crimes ranged from drug possession to petty theft, and he had been sentenced to the boy's correctional facility for stealing three hundred dollars.

Doran was the *Where's Waldo?* of trouble among the sixteen- to nineteen year-olds. If there was mischief in his dorm, he usually had something to do with it. He had been raised on the streets of a tough Detroit neighborhood, a chaotic microcosm that had imposed a fight-or-die mindset upon him. At the age of six, he'd been in a convenience store and had turned to put a coin into a gumball machine, when he'd heard a loud *bang*. He'd looked up to see his favorite cousin lying on the floor, dead with a bullet hole in his forehead and brains spilling out. Apparently, the cousin had flashed a gun at someone who had bumped him in line, but that other someone carried a gun, too.

My first meeting with Doran didn't last long. He

agreed to the session with a playfully defiant sense of innocence, acting as if the joke—and there was bound to be one—would be on the facility staff. He perceived his unlawful behavior, as most criminally minded young men do, through a cloudy lens of denial and minimization. In other words, he felt his life was going along just fine. The problem belonged to the cops, the courts, and the staff. The world, according to Doran, simply didn't understand that his crime was not really a crime.

"So, what got you placed here?" I asked over the lunch table. The meeting took place in the cafeteria because I didn't know Doran very well, and I wanted the kitchen crew handy in case he went off.

"Oh, man. It's bullshit. I mean, I took some money, and they say I stole it." Doran spoke openly and spontaneously, as if he assumed I would take his side once the facts were laid out on the table.

"How much did you take?"

"Three hundred dollars."

"You borrowed it?"

"No, man. I took it."

"So, you *stole* it?"

"No, man. . . . I took it from a drug dealer, man. The dude was a drug dealer."

"So when you steal from a drug dealer, that's not stealing?"

A look of anger and disdain spread across his face.

I leaned forward. "That's crazy thinking, Doran."

"What?"

"Your thinking's off. This is good. This is it. You got right to it. This is your criminal mentality. You're in it right now. You're lying to yourself. Stealing is stealing no matter who you steal from."

Doran violently pushed away from the table and stood up with his chest inflated and his arms flared out from his sides. I had a good fifty pounds and six inches on him, but I was still scared. He stood over me like he was going to give me a thrashing.

"That's it. We're done," Doran said with a snarl.

"That's okay," I said. "I don't want to work with anyone who doesn't want to work with me."

Doran turned and we began the long, tense walk back to the dorm. I provided the mandatory escort. Each step was slow, painfully silent, and tense.

I unlocked the dorm door and let Doran back in. It was quiet time inside, and one of the treatment counselors was seated near the entrance, watching over the boys. Several were sleeping. Some were reading books. Doran reentered his court-appointed home with a smile and a swagger, indicating that he had won a victory over the therapist. Doran's best dorm buddy flashed a cocky grin his way. I ignored the slight, wished Doran well, and retreated to my office and my computer. I sent an inter-organizational email to all relevant dorm staffers so they would be brought up to speed on Doran's behavior. Then I went home.

The next day, Doran, clutching several pages of stapled papers, ran up to me excitedly. He was upset.

"Will you sign this?" he blurted.

"What is it?" I asked.

"It's my level request. I need it for my level three. If you don't sign it, I can't go home and see my mom this weekend."

Doran seemed to be straining to keep himself from panic. The haughtiness that had filled him the day before was gone. He seemed torn between his pride and his goal of getting the prized "level three" behavior status and the subsequent visit home. His pride was now running a weak second to his desire to see his mother.

"If I sign it," I said, "that means I'm telling the dorm supervisor that you're interested in changing, Doran. I can't sign that because it wouldn't be true."

"You have to sign it. My mom's sick, and I have to go see her."

"Well, I don't want to keep you from your mother, but you showed me yesterday that you don't really want to look at your thinking or your behavior."

"You said you didn't want to work with me!"

"That's not what I said or meant. I said that I don't want to work with anyone who doesn't want to work with me, Doran. What you just said was another lie."

Doran ignored the confrontation.

"They say that I have to patch it up with you, or I can't go home on the weekend."

At that moment I realized what had happened. Tom Lutz had read the email about Doran's short, angry session. He had discussed it with other staff members and they agreed about not letting Doran go home as a consequence. It was a conscious action, a squeeze designed by Lutz to pinch Doran. Lutz and the other facility staff were channeling Dark Man energy, and they were requiring Doran to go down underground to tend his pots.

"I tell you what, Doran," I said. "I'll sign the paper without comment. But I will only do that if you agree to at least meet with me and take a look at your thinking."

"Yeah, I will," Doran quickly agreed.

I signed, and Doran triumphantly sailed out of the room. A cynical voice in my mind suspected that I had just been bamboozled.

My emphasis at this point in Doran's process, however, was *not* to enforce the agreement or to corner Doran. Lutz and the other staff members had already provided that luxury. My concern was to move fluidly in front of the young man—to be honest, to take emotional risks, to trust and be compassionate, even a bit vulnerable. It was my job to align the therapeutic goal of emotional and intellectual honesty with Doran's desire to see his mother. By naming the young man's pathological thinking and, simultaneously, modeling compassion, I was pulling him closer to me. *Work for me and things might go well for you*, I was saying in effect, *but you must be willing to go beneath the ground and tend the pots.*

Weeks later, Doran agreed to attend family group therapy sessions, despite his father's emotional and physical absence and his mother's track record of inconsistency. During one of the family group sessions, in which none of Doran's family members participated, I asked each person to talk about a time when they were very frightened. The purpose of this request was twofold: to get group members to break silence and to get the emotional energy moving in the room.

Most of the kids related stories of having been shot at, beaten up, or arrested. I took my turn by telling the group that my infant son had gone into surgery months earlier—a purposeful reference to an active father–son relationship.

"My most frightening moment was when they anesthetized my son for surgery," I said. "He weighed about fifteen pounds." I made a cradling shape with my hands. "They put him to sleep in my arms, and I had to hand the limp body of my son over to a stranger. I left the room knowing that they were going to cut him open. I went to the hospital cafeteria to order some coffee, but my wife had to order for me because I couldn't speak and keep from crying at the same time."

I offered this personal story intentionally as a conscious antidote to the other violent, crazy, fatherless stories.

Doran did not display any noticeable reaction to the story that night, but the next day, in a one-on-one session, the seed that had been planted sprouted. When I entered the room, Doran was unusually attentive and silent, waiting for me to get organized. I shuffled my papers around, trying to figure out what the heck I could possibly say to this young man that would make a difference. But before I could get started, Doran asked, "How's your son?"

I looked up to see a face that I hadn't seen before. The grief for his lost father weighed on his eyes. To be sure, Doran was sincerely concerned about my son, but his question was also about his loss, too. Suddenly, we had something in common.

"He's doing well," I replied. "He's kind of crazy in the morning, but cute. He gets up all grumpy, with his hair sticking up; takes me a while to get him laughing."

Doran wore an uncharacteristically grim look on his

face. He had turned. Overnight, he had begun to touch the yoke of grief that he had been carrying around his neck. It had been there all along, but he had finally allowed himself to feel it in the presence of a caring adult, specifically a caring adult male.

I softened my voice. "You know, Doran. It's very sad that your father promised to come see you here and then didn't." Doran's gaze shifted down and away, confirming that the arrow had hit its mark. "Doran, if you were my son, you would not be here alone. You'd have to shake me off. You'd have to work to get rid of me."

Doran turned his dazed expression back to the table and slowly nodded his head.

"You're smart," I continued. "You've got a great sense of humor. You're good looking. It's your father I really feel sorry for. He's really missing out on a great guy."

Tears began to well up in Doran's eyes, and he cried. At that moment, Doran had trusted and accepted a responsible adult into his emotional world. Most importantly, he had elevated his wounds to a conscious level, a pivotal step in the healing process for adolescent delinquents. At that moment, he knew he was hungry and lost. The two of us sat together and let the grief flow. It was Doran's turning point. He had begun the movement toward grief and emotional reconciliation. Lutz's "squeeze" had paid off. Doran was on his way down to tend his pots.

Creative Crises

In an article in *The Journal of Individual Psychology*, a periodical dedicated to the psychological thinking pioneered by Alfred Adler, a contemporary of Jung and Freud, Warren Rule illuminates the conventional wisdom of most schools of psychology: "[I]n their eagerness to be a positive influence in clients' lives, helpers may lose sight of the importance for clients to maintain an internal psychodynamic balance when confronted with the threat of change."[16]

The above suggests that consumers of psychological services must be, to a large extent, in control of the rate at which they confront their issues. While this is true for the depressed housewife or the neurotic husband, it does not apply for delinquent boys. For the typical adolescent delinquent, the therapeutic style has to be disruptive and directive. It is true that the therapist must be conscious of a delinquent's internal psychodynamic balance, but generally as a means to upset it.

In most psychotherapeutic relationships, clients are already anxious about their lives. They walk through the door of their own volition, motivated to "witness their own processes,"[17] to take their thought patterns out of their heads and examine them. Motivated clients hold their thinking in front of their own faces and study the details. Essentially, they hire therapists much as someone hires a gemologist. They want their thinking flaws examined. They want to know where the belief faults are and where any conclusions need to be polished.

Delinquent boys, on the other hand, flee from this kind of guided soul searching. Correctional facilities are populated by people who take their psychic and emotional pain out on others and don't want help changing course. Doran had been chased, handcuffed, and essentially dragged into treatment. In his book, the therapist and all the staff were enemies. It is the job of adolescent corrections therapists to wipe the mud from young men's eyes, so to speak, so that they can begin to see how their actions accentuate and worsen their own pain. But how does a therapist wipe mud from a young man's eyes?

The best opportunity to transform a boy comes through the facilitation of a controlled crisis. Here, Joseph Campbell quotes the nineteenth-century, German philosopher Arthur Schopenhauer:

We have to learn through experience what we are, want, and can do, and until then, we are characterless, ignorant of ourselves, and have often to be thrown back onto our proper way by hard blows from without. When finally we shall have learned, however, we shall have gained what the world calls character—which is to say, earned character. And this, in short, is neither more nor less than the fullest possible knowledge of our own individuality.[18]

If he had been considering delinquent males, Schopenhauer might have written: Because of blows from without, the delinquent male shall have gained the fullest possible knowledge of his individuality *and his own wounds*.

Incarcerated boys tend to stay unconscious until they weather a few blows from without and, paradoxically, begin to realize that the psychic and emotional wounds inflicted upon them in the past have been exacerbated by their own destructive behavior.

The ancient Greeks called this turning *epiphaneia*, or "striking appearance": the sudden realization, comprehension, or epiphany regarding the meaning of something.[19] Some delinquents realize they're lost when they're tackled and handcuffed by a cop; others when they are standing in front of a judge; still others when they spend their first night in a jail cell, and so on.

Expressions of Delinquency

Delinquency is spawned by many different causes and is expressed in different ways depending on the temperament of the individual. As a hypothetical example, let's say we discovered that Doran's mother had beaten him, *and* that his physiological makeup was resilient. We could then reasonably predict that certain synapses in his brain would have devoted themselves to aggression. Parts of his energetic brain that might otherwise have been dedicated to, say, competitive sports or academics would have formed a corridor of belligerence, so to speak. Neuro-passageways would have been constructed in his proactive mind and then paved with sharp stones and lined with briar patches in reaction to his mother's abuse. Violence would likely become a survival mechanism for an abused and resilient Doran. Love would have become equated with chaos, and he would have become a facilitator of that chaos throughout the community. Nature and nurture might have combined to create a burgeoning sociopath.

If, on the other hand, Doran's makeup was not resilient

and he had experienced the same hypothetically abusive mother, his brain would be more likely to develop
passageways directed toward depression or suicide.
This passive Doran would more likely collapse inward,
becoming self-destructive.

Doran was not, in fact, abused by his mother. He was
abandoned by an irresponsible and self-centered father
to a chaotic and lawless subculture. When a delinquent
father abandons his son in this way, the task of teaching the boy what it takes to be a man is relegated to
the mother, who is often attracted to irresponsible and
self-centered men. The son might then pick up from her
cues on how to become the type of man she is attracted
to. Doran learned from his father's example that men
abandon their wives and children, and that pursuit of
personal desire is more important than relationships. He
never had a chance to discover directly from witnessing
a responsible father's struggle. He never witnessed how
to walk upright in a masculine body. He simply never
had a good role model.

Through court records and information charted by
other staff members, we learned that Doran had only
met his father once. In that meeting, Doran's father
made it clear, by his behavior and attitude, that he was
not interested in having a relationship with his son. Nev-
ertheless, in a phone call, Doran asked his father to visit

him. To placate his son, the father agreed verbally, but never showed up. Doran's mother managed to appear for only a few family-visit sessions during his year of detention. To all intents and purposes, Doran had been abandoned to a correctional treatment facility by both parents.

With a new awareness of his family system, Doran began to put the heat on his parents for abandoning him. He peeked under the pot lids, slammed them down, and turned up the flame. When he understood that the abandonment was not his fault, he began to see his parents as they actually were. He did this by admitting that his father's promises were lies, and by acknowledging that his mother was not much better. He stoked the fires and turned up the emotional and psychic heat in his own gut by daring to be conscious.

His reward for shouldering the burden of consciousness, of course, was a bag full of ashes: his grief, a painful understanding of his family pathology, and a new *self-consciousness* about how messed up his thinking had been. But at least he was awake, and he could begin to walk as a man.

Doran became a leader in his dorm, confronting others' abusive behavior and lies. The last we heard of him, he was back out in the world and doing well. His ashes turned to gold.

Three

The Cycle of Shaping Delinquent Sons

TO DEVELOP HEALTHY EMOTIONAL INTELLIGENCE, TWO fundamental needs for a child must be satisfied. The first is the need to be loved. The second, less recognized and less understood, is the need to love. Both are equally important. It is the second need—to love the parent—that often requires young spines to deform, so to speak. Children contort themselves into a wide array of emotional shapes in order to admire and love abusive or neglectful parents. They often adjust their emotional expectations to make caring out of chaos and love out of abuse or neglect.

Robert Bly teaches us in *Iron John* that the key to a young man's passion lies beneath his mother's pillow.[20] To enter adulthood, the boy must take the key and unlock the wild aspect of his soul so he may enter the world of men and seize his passion. Many delinquent young men are afraid to reach for that key. They have no father to guide them, so they bend their spines all sorts of ways to maintain filial connections with their mothers.

Obviously, it isn't simply the absence of the father that leads to a delinquent son. Many single mothers raise boys who turn out quite well. Yet it is often the case that the mothers of delinquent boys have been abandoned by fathers themselves. We have already noted that many are attracted to men who are emotionally and spiritually absent. Many give cues to their sons, suggesting what a man should be. It's not that they consciously advocate pathology. It's simply what they are used to. A man who is actually responsible and assertive sometimes makes a father-abandoned woman feel uncomfortable.

Likewise, when delinquent boys act responsibly and reject pathological behavior, many of their mothers become anxious. In other words, if a delinquent boy were to examine his thinking and straighten out he would run the risk of upsetting his mother, who is often the most important person in his life. These young men frequently choose love partners like their mothers, as well. And the wheel turns. This is one of many ways pathology is passed from generation to generation.

Kenshin

Consider now a delinquent young man who refused to turn up the heat beneath the pots—a boy whose wounds were so deep and profound that he bristled at the very thought of claiming the grief that he carried, a boy traumatized beyond his ability to comprehend.

Kenshin was seventeen years old, with braided hair and a perpetual, taunting grin. He had been locked up for shooting a gun into the air while at a party with a crowd of young people around him. I first saw him just after he had completed the facility's long admission procedure. He was in the initial, locked-up phase of his treatment program. He had been retrieved from his room by one of the staff and seated at a table near the time-out rooms. Part of my job was to complete a list of questions about the boy's family background.

"All right, Kenshin," I said, "how many brothers and sisters do you have?"

"No sisters or brothers."

"Father?"

"Met him once for a couple minutes, but never lived with him. Fuck 'im."

"Okay, so you're angry at your father," I said. "Then you lived with your mom?"

"Yeah."

"No men in the house?"

"Boyfriends. . . ."

"Who was responsible for discipline?"

"My momma," Kenshin mumbled while raising his face slightly upward and smiling. It was a catch-me-if-you-can expression.

"Did any of the boyfriends ever hit you or touch you sexually?"

"No, man." Kenshin sat upright, making a fist with his right hand in the air. "I'd kill 'em if they ever touched me."

"Right, okay. So, if your mom was responsible for discipline, how did she discipline you?"

"Whuppin."

"So if you did something wrong, you were spanked."

"Yeah, I got a whuppin. You know." He tilted his head dramatically to one side and flashed another insolent grin.

"Was the spanking excessive?"

"What?"

"Was the punishment appropriate? Were the spankings over the top or . . ."

"No, man. No. I acted up, and she'd give me a whuppin."

I progressed on down the list, asking questions about extended family, educational level, and the like. Then it occurred to me that "excessive," "appropriate" and "over the top" were all relative concepts. Kenshin had taken control of that part of the interview by rushing past the definition of "whuppin." I returned to the subject of discipline.

"So you say that your mother gave you 'whuppins'? Could you describe a typical whuppin?"

"A whuppin. . . ." Kenshin shifted around in his seat again, suddenly anxious. His voice grew angrier. "I told you. I'd do something stupid, and she'd give me a whuppin."

"Yes, I understand that, Kenshin. You've made that clear. But could you describe a whuppin to me? What happened? Did she hit your head, hang you out a window, slap you?"

"No, man." He leaned way back in his chair and took a deep breath. "She'd whup me with a cord."

"A cord?"

"Yeah, an extension cord, sometimes a belt."

"She grabbed you by the arm and whacked you with a cord?"

"No, no man. My cousins held my ankles and wrists."

"Your cousins held your wrists and ankles?"

"That's what I said. Ain't you listening?"

"Your cousins would hold you down against the ground by the ankles and wrists, and your mom would whip you with an extension cord?"

"No, man. They held me up," Kenshin said.

"You were standing?"

"No, man. They held me up." He made a motion with his hands as if he were tugging on two ropes tied to a wall.

"So they suspended you?"

"Yeah, that. They suspended me." He grinned, but this time his grin was weak and didn't last more than an instant.

"So you were held suspended above the ground, and then your mother whipped you?"

"Yeah." Kenshin turned his eyes to the corner of the room. "Naked."

"You were naked when this happened?"

"Yeah. We were all naked."

"All?"

"Yeah."

"So tell me if I got this right, Kenshin. Your mother would tell you and your cousins to strip—all naked— and then she would have several of them hold you by the ankles and wrists, suspended with your belly hanging down? Then she would approach you with an extension cord and whip you?"

"Right."

"All across the back?"

"Yeah, up and down."

I slowed and softened my voice.

"Who have you told about this?"

"No one. I mean, my cousins. My aunt knows."

"You've never told anyone outside of your family about this?"

"No."

"How often were you disciplined in this way?"

"Every day," he said.

"No, you didn't understand the question. How often did you get disciplined in this way?"

"Every day!"

"I'm sorry. I'm not making myself clear. I'm asking how often it happened. How often did your mother whip you with a cord."

Kenshin sat back in his chair and crossed his arms. "I'm telling you. It happened every day."

"You're telling me that you were stripped and whipped with an extension cord *every day*."

"From when I was about four or five, until I was seven. But it wasn't always me. Sometimes I'd do the holdin'."

"So you were required to hold your cousins while your mother whupped them, too."

"Yeah."

"Naked?"

"Yep."

"Every day?"

Kenshin lowered his eyes and nodded his head. I

didn't know what to say. I knew I had to control my reaction, but it was very difficult.

"How did that feel, to have that done to you every day?"

"It hurt, but it's for my own good. I acted up, and I got a whuppin."

Kenshin suffered from a paradox common to the delinquent mindset, one that we mentioned earlier. He took responsibility for the outrageous abuse he had received at the hands of his mother. Yet he had taken little or no responsibility for the way he had endangered others by shooting a gun while standing in the middle of a crowded party of teens.

"Did you cry?"

"What's crying gonna do, man? You still get whupped. Besides, you didn't want the others to see you cry. I don't cry." He rolled his head around and flashed one last fleeting grin.

We completed the interview, but the weight of Kenshin's story suffused the air. I took Kenshin back to his dorm and went straight to Lutz for guidance on how to proceed.

Child protection services were contacted, and a report was made. Lutz advised that the abuse Kenshin sustained would be *the* central focus of his treatment. Therefore, my first task would be to get Kenshin to understand that whipping naked children with wire cords is abuse and not discipline, and the particular type of abuse he sustained had an element of sexual humiliation mixed in. (None of Kenshin's female cousins were reprimanded in this way. Only the boys.)

It was probable that the shame Kenshin carried as a direct result of his daily abuse was a key element of his rage. Rage can be a muddle of shame, fear, and anger, and it certainly takes something like rage to shoot a gun while standing in a crowd of people.

My next meeting with Kenshin was in the lunchroom because, as was the case with Doran, I wanted other facility staff around should Kenshin react violently. After a few pleasantries, I broached the subject. I, once again, slowed the pace and softened my voice.

"Kenshin, we talked about how you were disciplined the other day, remember?"

"Yeah," Kenshin said with his signature, cocky smirk.

"You said that your mom required you and your cousins to strip naked and that you and the others were whipped with an electrical cord every day. Right?"

"Yeah."

"You said it was for your own good. Have you given that idea any thought?"

"I acted up, and she whupped me. Was for my own good. Yeah, that's what I said."

I took a deep breath and let it out slowly. "Kenshin, that was not discipline, what your mother did. It was abuse."

Somewhere in his bones Kenshin already knew it, for he didn't argue or require me to elaborate. His reaction was instantaneous. I had broken the family-silence rule, the family-system devotion to the lie. His eyes turned into slits of anger, glaring across the table. He pushed his hands out toward my face and cracked his knuckles—a threat, implying that someone was about to get hit.

"Are you mad at me?" I asked.

Suddenly, just as quickly as it arose, Kenshin's anger dissipated. The look of a pouting child took over his face. Then, as if his ego were being drained out of him along with his rage, he slumped down in the chair. I let the question lay for nearly two minutes of pure silence, waiting for Kenshin to move or to speak. But he did not. His arms were limp at his sides, his jaw slack, his eyes glazed over.

"I want to make sure, Kenshin," I said, "that you know that I'm not talking about who your mother is. I know that you love her. And I've met her. She is certainly a lovable person. I want to make sure that you understand that I'm talking about your mother's behavior. This is about what she did, not who she is."

Kenshin didn't move.

"Kenshin, do you understand?"

He remained limp, staring downward with a numbed expression on his face.

"Kenshin, if you want . . . if you don't want to do this, I can take you back to the dorm."

His head barely turned from one side to the other, indicating that he wanted to stay. Something deep inside of him knew it had to be said.

"It's okay to just sit here too, Kenshin. You can take as long as you want."

Kenshin sat in a slumped-down posture for well over five minutes.

"Kenshin, do you think I'm on to something?"

He answered no, with a weak turn of his head.

"Do you think that what she did helped you to become a better person?"

Kenshin barely raised his head and spoke in almost a whisper. "You can say anything you want. It don't mean you're right."

"Yes, I might be wrong, and you get to tell me so. But I do think that your mom, or anyone who whips children with extension cords every day, is not acting appropriately."

The session with Kenshin didn't go on much longer. I concluded that enough had been accomplished for one day. Kenshin was given a little more time to recover, and I accompanied him back to his dorm. The dorm staff was informed that Kenshin had done some difficult work and that he should be handled gently.

Not surprisingly, staff came to understand that Kenshin's misbehavior was the pain of his wounds squeaking out sideways. His behavior was also consistent with what had been modeled for him because, just like his mother, he punished everyone around him for how miserable he felt. He taunted several of his peers until they had to be physically restrained. He refused to cooperate with facility staff and teachers.

Just as the corporal was pursued by the Dark Man, Kenshin was pursued by the cops, the courts, and the treatment facility staff. Unfortunately, Kenshin, unlike the corporal, refused to go down under ground. He was frozen by the fear of a world without his idealized mother. As a result, he kept wandering in the forest, lost and hungry. He was able to tolerate a therapist's confrontation (barely), but he allowed the presence of a therapist only temporarily as an emotional comfort. He refused to become proactive, courageous, and conscious, at least as long as we knew him.

Warriors and Destroyers, Styles for Confronting Lies

Delinquent boys, as we have said, twist their spines and their thinking into all manner of contortions to normalize the abuse and chaos they have survived. Kenshin, for example, *had* to say that he deserved to be stripped, humiliated, and beaten. Otherwise, he would have had to release the sentimentalized mother ideal that he had constructed in his head and in his heart. Since his mother was the only consistent adult figure in his life, risking losing her by facing reality was unthinkable, even if it meant living a lie: the sort of lie that is a prism to see the world through; the kind of subconscious lie that is far more intricate and ingrained than a simple untruth.

Generally, for adults working with delinquent teens, there are two archetypes that are useful for confronting lies. They are the "warrior" and the "destroyer." The Dark Man uses both of them in the treatment of adolescent delinquents.

The warrior sets out to identify lies and attempts to crush them by taking control. The warrior takes over and imposes truthful action or structure. At least, that is the warrior's goal. Warriors are masculine in nature, although they are not necessarily men. Many police officers are warriors. The United States was a warrior nation during World War II, crushing Nazism and fascism, rescuing Europe with the Marshall Plan, and imposing a new political order on Japan. The archangel Michael, with his glimmering sword of truth, is a biblical archetype of the warrior.

In corrections treatment programs, the staff members who hold kids accountable are warriors—warriors who use both carrots and sticks. They grant privileges, assign penalties, and give lectures. A typical warrior statement might go something like this: "I'm going to tell you how you should change and how you should accomplish that change. If you mess up, I'll make you uncomfortable until you straighten out. If you do well, I will reward you."

Jungians propose that there is a shadow side or reverse manifestation of every archetype. This is certainly true in the case of the warrior. In corrections, the shadow warrior is the prison guard who feels superior by exercising power over another human being. He taunts prisoners and doles out punishments, but his greatest interest is in exercising power for power's sake. There is no desire for rehabilitation or concern for the welfare of the prisoner.

The second style of the confronter of lies is the destroyer. Unlike warriors, destroyers do not try to take control. They abhor lies just like warriors do, but they are less likely to impose truth upon anyone. Mental health professionals tend to be destroyers, listening and posing Socratic questions but leaving clients to reach for solutions on their own. Destroyers are more likely to rely on inquiry to facilitate change, rather than pontification. A corrections professional with a destroyer style will lay open his or her own mind and invite the client to penetrate it.

For instance, a destroyer might say, "I don't understand, Jimmy. You joined a gang that will beat you senseless as an initiation when you join, and that same group of boys will kill you if you leave the gang. And these guys are the people you trust most? Can you help me understand that?"

Destroyer energy is often considered a form of feminine power, although destroyers are not necessarily women. Dr. Martin Luther King, Jr. was the supreme example of a destroyer. He treated racial discrimination like a repulsive balloon and used truth as a pin, exploding the lie and leaving the liars to clean up the mess.

When a delinquent boy engages a destroyer therapist, he ends up having to articulate his own lies. Hearing one's own lies coming from one's own mouth is powerful medicine. The destroyer is often a trickster, knowing the answer but pretending to need elucidation.

The dark side of the destroyer, or the shadow destroyer, satisfies its own needs by fostering codependence. The shadow destroyer feels superior and special, but is actually enmeshed and codependent. He or she might say, "Tell me, Jimmy, about your problem. I can understand you like no one else can. You're special, and you need me, so I'm special, too."

In corrections, the two styles often conflict. Warriors tend to perceive destroyers as too touchy-feely, unable to provide enough structure or discipline. Destroyers, conversely, tend to perceive warriors as excessively hard, rigid, and cruel.

While each style has its virtues, they are supremely effective when used together. Warriors provide structure and impose necessary crises; destroyers facilitate emotional and psychic emergence. Warriors push; destroyers pull. And both are agents of the Dark Man.

Pete

Pete was a wiry, street-smart seventeen-year-old. When he entered the facility, he was barely able to function. He was suffering from a classic case of Post-Traumatic Stress Disorder (PTSD). While walking down the street one night with his brother and another boy, a group of rival gang members stepped out from behind a corner, yelled "bitches," and started spraying bullets from their guns. Pete's brother, sustaining a severe wound to the head, ended up brain damaged. The other boy was seriously wounded in the leg. Pete ran away and survived without a scratch.

He was later arrested for an unrelated issue, and it was lucky that he was. The trauma had left him haunted by voices. Unable to sleep, he experienced panic attacks, and was depressed, exhausted, and suicidal.

After being successfully treated by the facility staff, Pete emerged from his PTSD as an arrogant, violent trouble-maker. As soon as his symptoms subsided, he went from emotionally crippled to cocky. (Healers sometimes face the troublesome paradox that the people they empower may use that power in counterproductive ways.)

One day, Pete had gotten himself into a tussle with one of his peers in the recreation room and was asked by a staff member to settle down.

"Fuck you, bitch!" replied Pete to the counselor, puffing out his chest in a defiant stance.

Two more staff people entered the room, then another.

"This is bullshit, man. You shit! Fuck you!"

The other boys were ushered back to their rooms. (This is the first step to calming a raging teen, for it eliminates the possibility of a riot and removes anyone whom the boy might be trying to impress.) Pete found himself alone with four beefy primary counselors.

One of the counselors, John, took the lead. "Come on Pete, let's sit down and talk about this. If you're angry, we can work something out. Insulting people isn't going to help."

"Fuck you," Pete replied. "Fuck you, bitch!"

John tried several more times to calm Pete, but it

soon became clear that the young man was not going to back down. Finally, one of the counselors left the room and returned with a six-foot padded board with Velcro restraining straps.

John was in his mid-thirties, with the unmistakable physique of a weightlifter. He took Pete gently by the arm, "Come on, Pete. Let's just go back to your room and talk."

Pete jerked his arm away. "Fuck you, bitch! Don't touch me."

The three other counselors inched closer. Pete's hands formed two fists and he tensed up, preparing to fight. John reached out once more, grabbed Pete by the upper arm, and swung the boy around into a bear hug. The others dove in, and in an instant Pete had been subdued. They tilted him like a Christmas tree in February, and laid him gently onto the restraining board.

"Fuck you, bitches! Fuck you!" Pete turned his mouth upward and spit right in John's face.

They carried Pete to his room and laid him down on his bunk, still fastened to the board.

"Fuck you, man! Fuck you! Bitches! Fuck you!"

Someone handed John a tissue. As he wiped the slime from his face and hair, he said to the boy, "Pete, I'm sorry it had to come to this. When you calm down, we'll talk."

Leaving one counselor behind to monitor Pete, John

and the others left, closing the door behind them. Within minutes, as is often the case with boys who are restrained this way, Pete fell into a deep sleep. The staff let the other young men out of their rooms, and things returned to normal.

Pete's lie was that the world revolved around him and that his internal, emotional discord was more important than the communal good.

John was the warrior, confronting Pete's lie and restoring order. He imposed structure while remaining respectful and empathetic, and he used just as much physical force as necessary.

Now, enter the destroyer.

Pete and I met a day later for a one-on-one session.

"I read the report about what happened yesterday, Pete," I said. "Can you tell me about it?"

"Man, they disrespected me. I wasn't looking for no trouble."

Lutz teaches that a destroyer stands behind a boy, figuratively speaking, looking over his shoulder and whispering questions into the boy's ear. *What do you think you're seeing? Why do you think that happened?*

"How did they disrespect you?" I asked.

"It's just bullshit. It's just bullshit."

"I hear you had some trouble with John in particular. Can you tell me about that?"

"Yeah. The fucker. He don't respect me. He don't care about me. It's bullshit. He just wants to fuck me up."

"How does he want to fuck you up?"

"You know, always disrespecting me. He just wants to take his shot at me."

"Really?" I said. "Did I read the report correctly that you spit in his face?"

"Yeah."

"How did he retaliate? Did he smack you or twist your arm?"

"No."

"You spit in his face, and he didn't retaliate?"

"No man, no."

"Did he swear at you?"

"No."

"Did he say anything mean to you?"

"No."

I let several seconds lapse. "He didn't say anything?"

"He said he wanted to talk."

"Talk about what?"

"That he was sorry he had to do what he did, and I could talk with him when I calmed down."

"He said he was sorry?" I asked. "What was he apologizing for?"

"They put me on that board-thing and laid me in my bunk."

"And that was what he was apologizing for?"

"Yeah."

"Okay, so help me understand. John's the big guy, right? The guy with all of the muscles?"

"Yeah."

"The record says that you called him a bitch and told him to fuck off before he ever touched you. Is that right?"

"Yeah."

"So you swore at him, called him a bitch, and then you spit in his face?"

"Yeah."

"And he says he wants to talk and that he's sorry for having to restrain you?"

"Yeah."

I let another moment of silence set in. Pete looked around the room and then back.

"I thought you said he was out to get you?"

Pete smiled, getting the point.

"Okay," I continued. "So help me understand, Pete, *John* is out to get *you*?"

Pete laughed. He could see that it would be fruitless to defend his victim's mentality. The way had been cleared to talk about how poorly Pete handled the situation and that perhaps Pete owed John an apology.

John crushed the lie that Pete could behave like a brute, and then he imposed structure and restored order using warrior energy. He provided the luxury of calm structure for the therapist to effectively apply destroyer questions. The destroyer entered and had Pete articulate his thinking. Pete was slapped in the face by his own voice lying. Articulating his own pathology actually made him laugh, a form of turning up the heat on himself.

Spawning Lies and Victim's Choices

After an episode of abuse, a victim will subconsciously settle upon a survival or coping response. The choice is usually productive at the time and unique to the personality of the victim. For example, consider the variety of pathological responses Kenshin could have employed to cope with the humiliation he endured at the hands of his mother. He could have drowned his shame in alcohol. He could have committed suicide. He could have raged against his mother by sexually assaulting women. He could have become depressed, or he could have murdered someone (as opposed to shooting a gun in the air). The abuser commits the sin of the abuse, but the victim chooses his or her particular reaction, even when the victim is a child.

While it may seem a bit like blaming the victim to consider trauma reactions as choices, it is actually a form of empowerment. Consider a woman who has developed a deep depression after being sexually abused for some time by her father. If a therapist plants the idea that the father imposed the depression upon her, then her depression is, by implication, controlled by her father. It is far more empowering to separate the abuse from the chosen reaction. In other words, if the depression is a survival mechanism chosen by the woman when she was a child, then it is within her power to unchoose depression and to heal. Regardless of her father's past or present behavior, she alone holds the power over her emotional and psychic health.

Delinquent boys often blur this separation, albeit subconsciously. Their neighborhoods or families traumatize them and compel them to be violent and they often continue—well into adulthood—to use the past as a reference or rationalization despite the emergence of alternative choices.

In Kenshin's case, there would be no future for him as a mature community man until he was willing to choose a different response to the humiliation he endured. It was his responsibility to unchoose the understandable, yet false, construct that helped him survive his childhood. Becoming hardened, obstinate, and violent may have actually saved his life, but it was causing a lot of trouble for him as a young adult. He needed to unchoose his victim response and realign his thinking and subsequent behavior.

Punishment vs. Treatment of Delinquents

The classical punishment model for working with delinquents implies that incarceration frightens them enough or is uncomfortable or inconvenient enough to deter them from illicit behavior. Penalize them by taking away their freedom, the thinking goes, and they'll straighten out. The problem is it isn't true.

Many adolescent detention facilities have changed or are changing to a different model of working with delinquents. Instead of punishing them, they're looking to treat them. There are several good reasons for this migration to treatment, one being that punishment subdues delinquents for a time but doesn't fundamentally change them. Punishment works quite effectively to improve behavior while in the controlled environment. Correctional facilities, for instance, very effectively force delinquents to stand in lines and follow rules. But once the young men are released, it's anybody's guess what each individual will do.

Studies show that treatment models are more effective than classical detention environments at reducing recidivism.[21] This is because treatment programs are more likely to entice a delinquent to let go of his denial, to go downward into his emotions, and to grieve. Treatment programs are also designed to monitor actual changes in thinking and emotional development before each young man is let back out on the street.

Treatment programs take into account more than a delinquent's criminal history. They also monitor the nuances of each individual's childhood experiences and psychological state. One teen might be extremely functional and another extremely dysfunctional, for example, so their respective treatment plans would need to be approached from different angles.

Let's say, for instance, that a boy named Joey was ten when his father abandoned him. He remembers his father's brutal beatings and the times his mother got beaten up for trying to protect him. His teachers always became fed up with him because he was too restless. He never fit in at school with the other kids because he was so moody. If Joey were brought into court for a truancy violation, the punishment model would simply hold him for a time, and then release him and wait until he committed a serious crime. The treatment approach would evaluate him for PTSD, ADHD (Attention-Deficit/Hyperactivity Disorder), and depression, actively addressing the question, *How has this boy's past affected him?*

Or, let's say that Joey got into a knife fight and slashed someone's ear; then he stole a car and purposely smashed it into a tree. The punishment model would rightly incarcerate him for as long as the law allowed. But Joey would be bunking with the kid who stole the mini-bike and the other kid who stole a canoe paddle from Walmart. Though their crimes were different, Joey wouldn't be treated any differently. The punishment model paints with a wide and often inaccurate brush.

By contrast, the treatment model would evaluate how far Joey had fallen into a criminal mentality and adjust his treatment plan and status accordingly. The corporal's symbolic journey beneath the earth to tend the pots, his reemergence, the return to the Dark Man for mentorship, and the reclaiming of the gold are all metaphors for treatment mechanisms, mechanisms that require a conceptual understanding of a delinquent's history, environment, family system, and relative emotional and psychic makeup.

Four

Physical Changes

WHEN A YOUNG MAN FOLLOWS THE DARK MAN BENEATH
the earth, cooks himself, and then reemerges, literal
changes occur in that young man's body. The changes
are as physical as gravity, light, sound, or magnetism. And
they occur—just as there are three pots to be tended—in
three areas or "ganglia" along the spine. These ganglia—
or chakras—shift on an energetic level relative to transformed thinking, emotions, and behavior.

The first ganglion we will address is the creative
energy center of the lumbar region of the spine. Viewed
from the front of the body, this spot is located several
inches beneath the navel. It is associated with creativity, sex, and physical action. The second is the heart.
The heart is associated with emotion, and it is located,
as its name implies, within the soft tissue behind the
sternum. The third is vision, thinking, and memory. It
is located in the center of the forehead and is associated with thought, clarity of vision, and consciousness.

One might also conceive of these ganglia as *chakras*, the ancient Hindu term for these centers of energy.

The First Chakra: Sex and the Creative Force Ganglion

Imagine for a moment an explosive, pulsating light emanating from the lower belly. This is the creative ganglion.[22] When the sportsman rejoices in the art of the game, when a man is working with tools or having sex, the creative energy below his navel is energizing his body. Some martial artists call this the "sea of chi," or "ocean of power," because it is located in the very center of the physical body. Its energy is neither good nor bad. It is merely powerful and creative. Within this masculine, creative center are the drive and the facility necessary to penetrate and change the world. The masculine creative center empowers men to turn their ideas and dreams into physical reality.

The masculine creative force undeniably includes sex, but it is not limited to sex. D. H. Lawrence observed the following in response to the early twentieth-century Freudian claim that sex is the primary human motive:

Even the Panama Canal would never have been built simply to let ships through. It is the pure disinterested

craving of the human male to make something wonderful, out of his own head and his own self, and his own
soul's faith and delight, which starts everything going.
This is the prime motivity. And the motivity of sex is sub-
sidiary to this: often directly antagonistic.[23]

The paradoxical question is, therefore, if this masculine creative energy is so creative, then why are so many
young men causing so much destruction?

Boys and men have a great—and often unconscious—
need to feel potent and to blend their creativity with other
males. They are driven to be part of something, to feel
useful and competent within community structures. Yet
our communities are often poor at initiating young men
into those structures. As a result, many young men feel
isolated and impotent. In our society, the weight of manhood—accountability and dependability—has become
for many a heavy, ill-fitting yoke. Even entering into marriage and fathering a child—a central experience of manhood—has become a solitary affair in which many of our
young men, isolated and perplexed, stumble and fail.[24]

Young men need the guidance of older men to help
channel their creative force. Robert Moore cautions,
for example, that it is only since the dawn of modernity
that men have become crazy or deluded enough to think
that they can function in love relationships without mas-

culine solidarity.[25] It is that solidarity with other men, especially older men, that keeps boys and young men on a productive path.

A Native American acquaintance of ours tells the story of his initiation. He belongs to an Ojibwe community that still practices initiation. At age sixteen, while living on a northern Minnesota reservation, he was stopped by an uncle as he was walking to a friend's house. "It is your time," the uncle said. "Come with me." Without further explanation the old man headed straight for the woods, with the young man dutifully trailing behind.

The two walked a great distance through the forest, until the uncle was sure that the boy was thoroughly lost. They came to a tree stand that the old man had obviously prepared for the occasion. The young man was told to climb the stand, and on top he found a blanket and a pipe. "You are not to kill anything while you are here," the old man said. "If a mosquito lands on your arm, brush it away. If you get hungry, smoke the pipe. If you get thirsty, smoke the pipe. Everything that happens here is meant to happen." The old man left and did not return for three days.

Our friend speaks of those three days as a great test of his will, a profound initiation. His uncle purposefully marked the transition for him, a form of Dark Man transformation. The initiation was completed by a naming ceremony and ritual.

Of course, corrections facilities can't be leaving young men out in trees throughout our cities. The point is that initiation into and inclusion in something purposeful are essential to the young male psyche, and there is little of this happening in mainstream culture today. In most of Europe and the United States, men jump into the fire alone, simply by getting a job and assuming the financial burden of being a man. They know that they are supposed to bring in the money for the family and they are told that they are supposed to stay married and attend to their children in some way. Yet they are denied, or deny themselves, the opportunity to share with other men the joys, challenges, griefs, and pains of their lives.[26]

The ancient initiations often involved symbolic and transformative injuries of some sort, such as circumcision, or jumping from a tower with a rope tied to one's ankle. Today, many dispossessed young men turn to circles of other dispossessed young men—we call them gangs—which offer brutal and unrefined initiations. In many street gangs, boys are savagely beaten as a way of inflicting a similar kind of symbolic wound. The elders of the gang, often adolescents themselves, bind the new gang members into the circle of young males. They share pain and grief with each other, and they assume social responsibilities within the gang. They create the structure that the community at large has failed to provide.[27]

Michael Meade, in *Men and the Water of Life*, says, "If the boys [of a culture] were not initiated into manhood, if they were not shaped by the skills and love of elders, then they would destroy the culture."[28] They are like shotgun shells exploding without the container of a rifle barrel. They have no aim, no direction.

Alienated adolescents despise the institutions that they perceive have rejected or abandoned them. The seeds of this hatred, while quite obvious to adults, are contained in young subconscious constructs. Few delinquents are able to articulate or even imagine a productive and successful place for themselves in any adult community. It is not at all unusual to hear a delinquent young man proclaim that he has no need for a job, no desire to follow the law, and no vision of himself as a devoted marriage partner and responsible father. Yet he might be very adept at dealing drugs, committing crimes, and fathering children. So it is obvious that delinquent males do not lack energy or motivation. Their creative lumbar energy centers are quite active, and their creative energy is very actively directed toward doing something. Unfortunately, it is often directed toward attacking and disassembling the very structures and institutions that they perceive have failed to embrace them, or which they feel have abandoned them.

Luckily, contained in every human male body are

mechanisms designed to govern the explosive creative energy emanating from his belly. And that brings us to the next energy center.

The Second Chakra: The Heart Ganglion

In the physiological sense, the heart is a pump for blood. Energetically, however, it is the container for relationships, community, and emotion. It is in our hearts that we hold our friends and our loved ones. It is where we hold close to our love of work and our sense of community. The force emanating from this energy center is associated with caring, altruism, empathy, and compassion.

In his poem "Vacillation," William Butler Yeats speaks to the ecstatic nature of community feeling, the ability to come from the heart and the capacity to care about people you may have never met. He expresses the idea that being able to bless is associated with feeling blessed. No wonder rejected or abandoned young men are unable to bless. It is because they don't feel blessed by their families, their neighborhoods, or their communities.

Alfred Adler designated *social interest* (*gemeinschaftsgefuhl*) as the backbone of all psychic and emotional health. He considered concern for one's community and concern for other individuals to be the indispensable psychological ingredient.

Paradoxically, Adlerian theory implies that all neurosis shares narcissism, or lack of social interest, as a common element. Like raging two-year-olds, delinquent boys are concerned solely with their own needs—they couldn't care less about the world around them. Their hearts are shut down. Whoever gets between them and their desire gets hurt. They are almost complete narcissists. They feel unblessed, so they are, consequently, unable to bless.

When the adolescent male heart has been wounded by a lack of blessing, when a boy's physical energy is not governed by the compassion and empathy of the heart, his creative energy is then left ungoverned. The horses run wild, so to speak. He may have no feeling, or only distorted feelings, about what the great force inside his belly drives him to create. Chances are that he will create chaos and discord, and he will lack the capacity to evaluate his creations on any empathetic or sympathetic level. Worse yet, he may purposely hurt others to compensate for his emotional dysfunction.

The Third Chakra:
The Vision Energy Center

The brain, with its hundred-billion neurons, forms patterns in response to the messages received from the five senses. Each teen walks with a veritable cosmos inside his head. The "brain" is the physical organ held within the skull, and the "mind" is the construct created by the brain. Identity and worldview form the lion's share of what we call the mind.

The part of the brain that is responsible for higher brain functioning—conscious thought, reason, calculating, language, etc.—is the prefrontal cortex. In evolutionary terms, this part of the brain is quite new. It is the center of how we think, and it comprises 80 percent of the brain's mass.[29] With an estimated ten-to-the-millionth power of "on-off" patterns, the brain fashions itself into that which we call the personality[30]—an individual brain's way of thinking. The mind or personality, then, dictates an individual's lifestyle.[31]

Using an arsenal of sophisticated brain imaging equipment, researchers are now beginning to prove something long presumed by many: the developing human brain is, to a great extent, shaped by interpersonal relationships.[32] Relationships, especially parental ones, compel specific parts of the brain to activate, refine, and develop. In other words, the behavior of childhood caregivers actually helps govern the *physical* formation of electrochemical passageways in the brain. Our relationships serve as the civil engineers of our internal cerebral landscapes, building bridges, redirecting streams, and erecting dams.

In *addition* to the empirical fact that nature makes us who we are, we can now proclaim with certainty that our physical brains are formed partly in response to the values, priorities, and behaviors of our childhood caregivers. As far as the nature–nurture argument goes, this evidence shows that our personalities are formed by a mixture of both: "Development is a product of the effect of experience on the unfolding of genetic potential. The swing [of the theoretical pendulum] . . . to either the genetics end or the experience end can lead to erroneous conclusions."[33]

It is rare that a child emerges from the womb a juvenile delinquent. It is essential, then, that mental health workers, teachers, social workers, and adolescent corrections professionals consider a young man's background, his childhood environment, and his family system in addition to his brain chemistry and psychological temperament.

Just as the vertebrae must be aligned for optimum physical health, the three energy centers must be aligned and functioning properly. While the heart is required to monitor the creative force pulsating beneath the navel, it is the brain and its esoteric construct—the mind—that is the monitor of both lower functions.

Five

Brain Sequences

MANY LIBERAL ARTS COLLEGES MANDATE THE LEARNING of second languages. This class requires students to struggle, word by word, until speaking French, Spanish, Italian, or for that matter Ojibwe becomes second nature. The young delinquent mind that has been transformed develops new behavior sequences in a similar way. Time spent below the earth sweeping ashes and tending pots allows the creation of new pathways in the brain.

Humans are blessed (and cursed) with a varied and intricate emotional range. We distinguish the subtle differences between joy and contentment, love and lust, anger and rage, and sadness and grief. Shame, for example, is generally experienced as one's feeling bad about one's character, whereas guilt is feeling bad about one's behavior, and so on. These complex distinctions allow us to manage very complicated communal structures and to sustain longer-lasting and more secure social connections.

Our emotional experiences are often the result of context. In other words, societal mores and customs influence our emotional expressions. A smile in Bangladesh might mean someone is very frightened or nervous; grieving is circumspect and restrained in Oslo; men sometimes cry in Palermo to express happiness; and so on.

The myriad emotional distinctions often lead to confusion and discord. Some are subtle; some are not. For instance, responding violently may be acceptable and serve a man well if he is in danger. But if he sees peril where there is none, he may actually create it. He may perceive, for instance, his wife's infidelity as a threat to his existence. If she leaves, he believes he will be emasculated. He misreads the pain and embarrassment he feels as a threat. Instead of grieving and moving on, the man believes he has to crush the danger. He responds with aggression as if his life depended on his ability to control his wife, and so on. Where there is emotional confusion, so there is psychic turmoil; where there is psychic turmoil and distorted emotional expression, so there is social chaos.

Another common emotional distortion is in the man who feels sad or useless and concludes he needs danger as a way to stimulate himself. He may steal a car or break into a house. We know of someone who used to break into houses to watch people sleep. He never stole anything and there was nothing sexual about anything he had ever done. Another individual stole cars and raced them down the highway, only to throw them in reverse at high speeds and then run away. He never made a dime from stealing a car, yet he stole many.

Emotions Out of Sequence

When we're afraid, we either attend to what is frightful or we move away. This is commonly referred to as the fight-or-flight response. Like the analogy of fingers touching a hot stove, if something causes pain we move it out or we stay away; much like radar is to a ship at sea, fear and pain enable us to safely navigate the world.

Conversely, we are attracted to situations and people we perceive as pleasing. We see our friends and loved ones, and we feel safe. We feel calm in the places we are comfortable, and we let down our guard. Positive and negative emotions and their corresponding physical responses have enabled the human species to survive and maintain its complex social structures.

These human emotional responses are governed by two basic sequences. The first is the *stimulus* ➜ *limbic* ➜ *body* series. From an evolutionary perspective, this progression has been very valuable because it allows for quick reactions to dangerous situations. Impulses reach the amygdala in the limbic region of the brain before we have time to think. Reaction is instantaneous. We have all experienced this when someone startles us by jumping out from behind a corner or when the monster suddenly appears in the horror movie. We react immediately. The body readies itself for fight or flight in a split second.

The second emotional response sequence is more complicated and slow. It is the *stimulus* ➔ *limbic* ➔ *prefrontal cortex* ➔ *body* series. This sequence includes the prefrontal cortex, allowing for thought about context, meaning, and anticipation of consequence. When a child says that you look old or fat, for example, you might be aghast, but your prefrontal cortex enables you to consider the source. You consider that a child is speaking, and that she or he doesn't realize what she or he is saying. You might then consider a range of responses that maintain social equilibrium.

Most adolescents who chronically break the law have grown up in dangerous family situations. Many of them have been sexually, emotionally, or physically abused, and many have witnessed significant abuse perpetrated by or against other family members. They have learned to use the *stimulus* ➔ *limbic* ➔ *body* sequence as a quick and effective means of defense. This sequence excludes the judgment function of the brain and is often the only form of stress response known to a delinquent teen.

In dangerous households, the most profound casualty is trust. Abused or neglected children won't go to other people for comfort, and, consequently, they live emotionally isolated lives. Instead of reaching out to other people who might make them feel better (due to the excretion of dopamine in their brains), these boys and young men often opt for the adrenaline high of a fight or high-risk behavior. Adrenaline can be a coping substance just like alcohol or any other drug. As such, these adrenaline fixes may actually help a young person persevere through difficult times. Some delinquents pick fights, break the law, and engage in risky behaviors simply to cope with their emotional and psychic wounds.

Impulsives and Adrenaline Junkies

All delinquents suffer from one shared affliction: they lack the ability to regulate and express emotion productively. Furthermore, all lost and hungry young men fit loosely into three general categories in this regard. The three groups are the *impulsives*, the *adrenaline junkies*, and the *impulsive adrenaline junkies*.

Impulsives
This group comprises boys and young men who chronically engage in rash behavior. They react with impulsive

aggression when angry. They don't think about consequences or the damage they inflict upon themselves or others as a result of their recklessness. It is difficult or impossible for them to delay gratification. If they need money one minute, they may very well shoplift the next. If something is in their way, they break it down. If behavior is a form of communication, these young men are screaming that their prefrontal cortexes are not being used.

Impulsives are eminently treatable. The main goal, simply put, is to engage the prefrontal cortex into the reactive sequence. That goal can be realized by emphasizing long-term goal orientation while encouraging active catharsis of unexpressed grief. Once an impulsive delinquent owns his own long-term goal and grieves his wounds, his pathological thinking and behaviors can then be reframed as remnants of the past and obstacles to his future.

Adrenaline Junkies

This group is comprised of youngsters who thrill-seek and/or create drama in illicit ways. The young man mentioned earlier who broke into houses to watch people sleep and the guy who ruined cars for fun are both adrenaline junkies. Adrenaline junkies commit crimes or create discord to access the high that adrenaline provides. They get charged by generating chaos, dissension, or fear in themselves, others, and the community at large. They get high by fleeing the police and romanticizing themselves after they commit a crime or start a fight. They don't fight out of anger necessarily; they fight for the rush. They may also manipulate others to create drama. They may push others' emotional buttons and then sit back and enjoy the buzz.

The prognosis for delinquent adrenaline junkies is not as good as for impulsives. There is an element of malevolence to this kind of mindset. The treatment mechanisms are much the same as dealing with impulsives, but with the added aim of convincing the individual that a dopamine high (meaningful connection with another human being, and pride in socially relevant behavior) feels better, is more productive, and is far more sustainable than the adrenaline rush of destructive or anti-social behavior.

Impulsive Adrenaline Junkies

This group is comprised of individuals who suffer both of the above afflictions. Impulsive adrenaline junkies lead extremely chaotic lives and tend to be at the highest risk of re-offense among all delinquents. Subsequently, they require the largest amount of intervention, supervision, and structure.

Male and Female Brains

Author L. Frank Baum produced one of the most powerful metaphorical stories in the twentieth century—*The Wonderful Wizard of Oz*. The story's protagonist, Dorothy, is required to fight her dark animus—The Wicked Witch of the West—who personifies her malevolent, inner, masculine potential. In terms of "The Devil's Sooty Brother," Dorothy is required to cook not the pots but herself and find her heart (the Tin Man), her creative potential (the Lion), and her clear vision (the Scarecrow). As Baum describes it, Dorothy's world is transformed from one of banality ("she could see nothing but the great gray prairie on every side. . . . The sun had baked the plowed land into a gray mass . . . the house was dull and gray as everything else") to one of emotional and psychic depth, represented by Oz and its color ("lovely patches of greensward . . . banks of gorgeous flowers . . . birds with rare and brilliant plumage"). Baum created a wonderful archetype for young women and girls.

"The Devil's Sooty Brother," however, tells this story of growing up in a different way—with a male shamanic figure and a male protagonist. Impotent Oz would have done little for our lost and hungry young lads. The physical and psychological foundations of males and females are different. In women's brains, the connector between the two hemispheres, the corpus callosum, generally has a greater "bandwidth," as it were, than in the brains of men. This enables women's brains to complete multiple functions at once and to better understand and bridge the verbal and abstract worlds.

A woman, for example, is more likely to notice subtle cues in her relationships, ones that a man is likely to miss. She will be more sensitized to faint relational nuances, the little intimations indicating whether she is being valued or disrespected. She is more likely to have strong emotional—and even physiological—reactions to her environment, too. Some theorists maintain, for instance, that before the time of electric lights, women menstruated in relation to the phases of the moon. Because of this connectivity to her environment, a woman is more likely to use her emotional strength as a guide. The heart rules. She will tend to feel first and then create according to how she feels, as opposed to men, who tend to distinguish how they feel according to what they've created. Additionally, several specific biochemical agents make females different from men. One is the hormone oxytocin. Oxytocin is nicknamed "the cuddle hormone." Adolescent girls experience surges in oxytocin, as well as estrogen. These account for their drastic mood swings.

Dr. David Walsh, a nationally recognized expert on the adolescent brain, tells the hypothetical story of an adolescent girl sitting at the dinner table with her family.[34] The mother, for the sake of conversation, asks the girl to talk about her day in school. The girl screams that she is not a trained parrot, she's sick of being nagged, and she hates the whole family. Then she storms off to her bedroom and slams the door behind her. Within a matter of minutes, this same girl is curled up on her bed, running a surge of oxytocin, cuddling with her stuffed animals.

Conversely, in males, the creative force below the belly rules. The great testosterone factory in men's testicles stimulates a broader visual function. It also creates larger muscles and skeletal frames, a stronger drive for sex, and a tendency toward aggression. Because of the last, men tend to be territorial. In adolescent males, the explosion of testosterone occurs before the brain is fully developed. Dr. Walsh likens adolescents to cars that have souped-up engines and faulty brakes.[35]

To illustrate how precious testosterone is to male potency, we need look no further than the alternative: men with artificially lowered testosterone levels. Depo-Provera is a common birth control pill that contains a synthetic version of the female hormone progesterone. In men it reduces testosterone production, which makes it a good drug for treating sex offenders. When administered properly, Depo-Provera reduces the likelihood that sexual predators will re-offend; when it is improperly prescribed and given in large doses, however, the testicles produce almost no testosterone. Men who are over-medicated in this way become apathetic and totally lacking in any desire. Their world becomes flat, and they become depressed, hopeless, and numb.

Six

Transformed Men

RICK MET WITH ME AT A RESTAURANT BOOTH IN A MINNE-apolis bistro. He was twenty-two-years-old at the time of the interview, a well-built, handsome fellow with penetrating eyes, a serious demeanor, and a reluctant smile. His hair was meticulously groomed, his manners were refined, and his speech articulate. He showed up ready to talk about his history of trouble with the law.

In many ways, the story Rick told was typical for delinquents. His parents divorced when he was two. His father had abandoned the family. He, his brother, and his mother moved from home to home. At a very young age Rick started stealing car stereos and found it to be an easy and quick way to make money. His placement in juvenile corrections was for breaking into and burglarizing cars.

"I was ten years old, and I hadn't seen my dad for over half a year," he began. "We didn't know where he was living at the time. I was driving down a freeway north of Chicago with my mom and my brother. I looked out of the window, and there was my dad, driving the car next to us. After that, we knew he was in town, so my mom tracked him down and got hold of him. My brother and I started to see him then, but not long after that he announced he was moving to Florida."

"Do you think your dad's absence had anything to do with you getting into trouble?" I asked.

"No. It made no difference. It was more what my mom taught me. She made the difference."

"But after you started heading in the wrong direction, who made the difference? Was it your placement? Do you think it was the facility that turned you around?"

"In many ways, the placement taught me to be a better criminal," Rick said. "You make friends with the guys on the inside because you get so lonely, and breaking with friends is key."

"But didn't anyone there make a difference? In the story 'The Devil's Sooty Brother,' the Dark Man tricks the lost boy into going down into his emotional baggage. In your case, it would mean looking at your family and your pain. Didn't you meet anyone like this?"

Rick nodded enthusiastically, "Yeah, it was my primary, Jennifer."

A "primary" is a corrections professional who works

one-on-one with delinquents, acting as a disciplinarian, monitor, and counselor.

"So in your case, the Dark Man energy came to you through a woman."

"Yes. She listened to me. She was kind of like a parent."

"Were you able to acknowledge that you had a problem and needed to take a look at your thinking? Did that happen at the juvenile detention center?"

"No, it didn't. When I was released I stole again."

"But do you think that if you weren't placed, you'd still be a thief?"

"Oh, yeah. I would. I needed someone to stop me. And two of my friends betrayed me, so I started to look at who I was loyal to. I guess I always had a conscience. I just never listened to it."

"You seem to be proud of being honest now."

"I am. Sometimes it's hard to face the week with $20 in your pocket, but you always know that check's coming on Friday."

"That feels good, doesn't it?"

"Yeah. My fiancée and I have a six-month-old daughter. That's the reason. We're getting married, and I paid for the ring with the money I earned. No one can say that it didn't belong to me."

Rick expresses humility here—the willingness, as "The

Devil's Sooty Brother" would have it, to wear a smock. He is now proud of his honesty and work. In the form of a loving wife and beautiful daughter, he has inherited a kingdom.

Giving Back

John Turnipseed is a man many had given up on. From the time that he was a boy until he reached his thirties, John was either hanging out on the street, committing crimes, or he was incarcerated. An early incarnation of the Bloods gang in Minneapolis was essentially his extended family. This gang is believed to be responsible for at least twenty murders.

John has been convicted of armed robbery, burglary, and a long list of other crimes. As a juvenile he spent time at several boys' detention centers and treatment centers. As an adult, he was sentenced three times to adult prison. Yet today, at fifty-six, he is the director for the Center for Fathering in Minneapolis. He is a Baptist minister and a devoted husband and grandfather. He told his story during a series of interviews at a Minneapolis restaurant.

"I believe that my story can help others, so I want you to use my name," he insisted. "I spent the first five years of my life in Selma, Alabama. My life there was good. I had two grandmothers living nearby, my father sang in the church choir, and I had relatives living all around me. I had never been in a fight.

"We moved to Minneapolis in 1960 and then every day I had to fight. Because of my accent and the fact that I was new in town, I was getting beat up all the time. Then one day, my older cousin, Tommy, intervened and taught me how to take care of myself. 'Show me the kid who beat you up,' he said. He handed me a stick and told me to go over and hit him with it. I hit the kid over the head, and he ran away crying. Tommy had taught me how to retaliate, and it felt good."

For the first time since his family moved to Minneapolis, John experienced some degree of power over his surroundings, and a feeling that he could defend himself. He learned that retaliation in the form of violence was an effective tool for avoiding being humiliated.

"Eventually, I was fighting all the time, but I learned that it wasn't enough *just* to fight. You'd have to pull me off of the guy. I wouldn't stop. I'd keep kicking him in the groin, whatever. That way I'd only have to fight once a week rather than every day. I got a reputation, and my reputation made it so others would think twice before starting something with me."

Before he was ten, John had taken his older cousin's lesson and cultivated it. He learned that his tough reputation could be used effectively for something beyond defense. He came to realize that intimidation could be used as a means to attain authority. Not only did the fear he instilled in others protect him, but he began to see that his family was protected by his reputation as well.

"My siblings didn't have to fight as much as I did because they were my siblings. They'd say, 'That's Turnipseed's brother. Don't mess with him or you'll have to face John.'"

John tells how his cousin Tommy was eventually shot dead at age twenty as he attempted to retaliate on John's behalf.

"Some guy threw lye soap in my eyes. Tommy went over to his house to stick up for me. He went in and they shot him dead. I was fifteen then. And while all of this was going on, everything at home had fallen apart. My dad started drinking and hanging out with drug dealers, gamblers, and womanizers. It only took him about one-and-a-half years to complete the slide. Eventually, he began to beat my mother.

"In one of my placements, they misdiagnosed me as ADHD," John explained. "I was exhausted because I was staying up all night to protect my mom. My dad would get home late at night, all hours of the night, and I knew he was going to beat her. So I'd stay up all night. I was the only person there to protect her. They thought I had ADHD.

"One day, I was sitting in the car with my dad. I knew that he kept his gun under the front seat. I was getting pretty tough by then, and he knew it. I said, 'Dad, don't reach for your gun, but I've got something to say to you. If you ever hit Mom again, I'll kill you.'

"His hand began to go down a little toward his gun. I said, 'Don't do it, Dad, because you know I will kill you.' I figured I'd do five, maybe seven years for killing him, and I was willing to do it to protect my mom. And he knew that I would. After that, he never hit her again."

At age eighteen, John was introduced to crack cocaine. Soon afterward, he became involved in crime with extended family members. They evolved into a gang and called themselves the Bloods. (They were not the Bloods from California; they called themselves the Bloods because they were all related. When the California Bloods actually came to Minneapolis, John's family inherited their enemies—a sad coincidence of nomenclature.) Much of the gang's activity centered on crack-cocaine use and distribution.

"They caught me burglarizing homes and sent me to the County Home School. There was a golf course next to the place," John said, noting the irony with a shake of his head. "The shop teacher there was a pregnant woman. She made fun of my name, you know, Turnipseed, apple seed, something like that. I picked up a knife and went after her. And I was going to kill her. It took five guys to stop me. Then I was off to Red Wing Correctional Facility. Then others. I graduated to armed robbery, assault, violent crimes. I was sentenced to St. Cloud [State Penitentiary] in 1973, Stillwater [State Prison] in 1980, and Stillwater again in 1984. The most dangerous thing I learned in prison was Transactional Analysis. They taught it to me as a form of treatment, but it basically taught me how to fool people better. I learned how to look good even though I hadn't changed.

"That was back in the days when inmates had a lot of leeway in the prisons. Because of who I was and my reputation, I had a lot of power. I had a cell. It wasn't the cell where I stayed. It was more like an office. One day, I walked in and two of my crew were raping a guy. Because I was the leader, the guy begged me to make them stop, and I could have. But I just walked out. They hurt him really bad. Later, I saw them marching the two guys who did it away. You know, two black guys rape a white guy. It was a big deal. Most of the inmates were white."

While in prison, John developed a high level of competency with computers. When he was released, he applied for and got a job teaching computer skills to handicapped people. The job was a pivotal factor in John's life. For the first time, people were respecting him for his brains and talents, not out of fear. He was empowering weaker people, as well, rather than preying on them. Empathy and compassion became integral parts of his worldview.

John acknowledged, however, that while part of his conscience had begun to emerge, part of his soul was still asleep. With his new skills, he had evolved into a white-collar criminal. He used his skills to create a burglary ring, and he was caught.

"It was the first time I ever felt shame," John said. "I felt ashamed in front of my students. I felt ashamed because of the people who trusted me and gave me the job."

Once again, John was facing prison time. This time, however, a series of characters intervened. John firmly asserts that his faith saved him.

"It was the power of Christ," John said. "There was this prosecutor who just wanted to put me away, and he was replaced that very day by this Christian prosecutor. The probation officer was on my side, and my mentor, Art Erickson (Urban Ventures founder and CEO), was there. They all convinced the judge that I deserved another chance."

John reports that the police harassed him for quite a time after he had truly straightened out. They were unconvinced that he had changed until they finally caught another man who had committed crimes of which John was accused. They subsequently put out the word to the other Minneapolis cops that John's transformation was genuine.

These days you'll find John in his South Minneapolis office, organizing outreach groups who intervene in the lives of troubled kids. Once a month, he preaches at Central Church. John is no longer hungry and wandering in the forest.

"You could say that I work with the least, the last, and the lost," he said with a smile. "When they find a lost person, they bring that person to me.

"You see, you've got to be careful not to create psychopaths. When a kid becomes used to trauma, and causing trauma is modeled as a way to gain power, you're going to create psychopaths. And if you carry a lot of shame about who you are, if you truly believe you are worthless, that power will insulate you from that shame. You see, you want a kid to run home crying when he's hurt. If he doesn't run home crying, then there's something wrong.

"Whole groups of these young guys go into prison unloved, un-fathered. This confirms what they've already been told, that they are shameful, worthless, and unloved. Then, to prove they are unloved, they come out and can't get a job. A job *is* love. These kids are the most vulnerable. They are just scum to the world, and being without a dad is the number one indicator of failure. The father is the one who keeps the wolves away."

"What about gangs?" I asked.

"What many people say about gangs is untrue. Gang members don't belong to the gang to get family needs met. They don't get their emotional needs met, their need to belong and all of that. That's a bunch of bull. They belong to gangs so that they can use each other. They don't care about each other. And having people fear you to protect your family, that's a bunch of garbage, too. It's all about power and fear. I did the things I did because I wanted to feel powerful and avoid the fear. I might have pretended I was protecting my family, but I was avoiding the fear and going for the power for myself."

"What about the Dark Man energy? Who reached out to you when you were young and lost? Who compelled you to stir the pots?"

"I remember two people, especially, who managed to get through to me. One was Father Capucci, the chaplain at Red Wing Correctional Facility. I behaved when he was around because I knew he loved me. He was the only man I allowed to hug me. The other was a teacher there, Mr. Drewes. He made a deal with me that he would teach me how to lift weights if I'd study and pass my GED."

"How do you see the role of religion?"

"We've gotten rid of the Bible. This has devastated the African American family. If you look carefully, you'll see that when a gang-banger makes a real conversion, they [other gang members] respect that. You can see the guys in their suits and ties with their bikes going through the toughest neighborhoods, and nobody touches them. It would take a couple of minutes to steal their bikes and that would be a hit of crack, but nobody does it because the Bible is still respected.

"I can put this in words for the non-religious. When I'm talking about Jesus, I'm talking about fathering and father figures. I'm talking about being unconditionally accepted rather than rejected and shamed. I'm talking about a structure that appeals to a young person's conscience rather than his fear. And of course, I'm talking about love. An unconditional love like Father Capucci showered on me."

"What about drugs?"

"Crack cocaine is the worst thing that has ever happened to the black community," John said. "We survived slavery. We survived Jim Crow and racism. But crack cocaine is the only thing that can get an African American mother to abandon her children."

"But what about the paradoxical way women are depicted and treated on the street?" I asked.

"As far as the treatment of women, it takes on two forms. The mother is the only one that's always there for you. She becomes of overwhelming importance. She is the beginning and the end. On the other hand, when you're living this kind of life, you believe that you *have* to exercise power over whomever you can. So women, women other than your mother, become objects that you can have power over, and you exercise that power because you can. That's why there is such a contradiction between how delinquent kids worship their mothers but degrade women in general: 'whore,' 'bitch,' and all of that."

Of all the ashes that have turned to gold, conscience appears to be the most prominent of John's gifts. Through courage, persistence, his faith, and a little help from some others, he managed to cook himself into an exemplary community man.

Ironically, of all the crimes he committed, John is haunted most by one that he didn't even commit.

"When my conscience was still asleep, I was out with one of my friends. This old woman was standing there waiting for a bus. My friend decided to take her purse, and when he did he threw her down way hard. He was really rough with her. We went to a friend's house nearby, and pretty soon there were cops all over the place. Another friend went to see what it was all about, and he came back to say that the old woman had died. Even though I didn't do it, to this day I still can't drive down that street. My friend did time for that, but I still think of that old lady. I could have stopped it, but I didn't. Her life shouldn't have ended that way."

Seven

The Healthy Family, the Teacher, and Meeting the Princess

WITH SO MANY YOUNG CORPORALS WANDERING AROUND lost and hungry in the urban forest, one is compelled to ask why there are so many delinquent boys. Where are they all coming from? Why is there a need for Dark Man wisdom?

Chaotic families and AWOL fathers are the main cause of male adolescent delinquency. Most dysfunctional families of delinquent teens are dysfunctional for obvious reasons—domestic violence, drug and alcohol abuse, parental neglect and abandonment, etc. Much has been written about these pathological families, but far too little has been written about what constitutes a healthy family.

A crucial component of healthy families is connectedness, an element that requires children to be emotionally bound to parents and to circles of caring adults. These adults must include both male and female elders who are involved with the children on a regular basis. The ideal circle might include aunts, uncles, grandparents, neighbors, teachers, involved professionals, coaches, clergy, family friends, etc.—adults who admire and bless the children. These elders can also admonish poor behavior. Clearly, healthy families are not solely the result of being led by two parents of different genders. For boys especially, though, the active participation of male role models is absolutely necessary to contain them and help them thrive.

University of Minnesota researcher David Olson and his colleagues have created a model that measures the health of family systems by placing them on a cohesion/flexibility scale. Olson's model suggests that healthy families exhibit a balance of cohesion along with a balance of flexibility.[36] Too much flexibility, for example, and the family environment becomes chaotic; not enough flexibility and it becomes too rigid. On the other axis, too much cohesion and the family becomes enmeshed; too little cohesion and the family falls apart.

The family systems of delinquent boys tend to be at least two standard deviations from balance, or the ideal for a healthy family. In other words, they are often flexible to the point of chaotic, and they are disengaged and/or enmeshed.

Healthy families are able to accommodate normal developmental changes. They are able to hold together throughout the phases of each member's lifespan, starting from infancy, through adolescence, adulthood, and well into old age.[37] Healthy family systems provide the emotional flexibility to process conflict, and to adapt in the face of unforeseen events and traumatic experiences.[38] They have lucid boundaries between individuals and generations.[39] While healthy families respect privacy, they avoid the shame and tension that often result from family secrets. Family members are allowed to speak the truth the best that they know it.

Healthy families tend to avoid double binds.[40] A boy is not forced to choose between consciousness and his mother's love. He is allowed to name inappropriate behavior without the risk of being shunned. Above all, he is not required to shut down his emotions to survive. Healthy families avoid creating these dilemmas.

Healthy families also provide containment and structure for their children. Discipline is appropriate and restrained, yet it is omnipresent. Adolescents are required to demonstrate competence in other areas of their lives (school, church, Boy Scouts, etc.) before being allowed independence.

A Healthy Family Is Like the Sun

Here is one teacher's model for a healthy partnership. The great expanding sun, with its exuberant masculine force of nuclear fission, blasts out in all directions. Opposing this powerful expansion is the great contracting force of gravity, the sheer attraction of matter to itself. Without the great feminine power of gravity, the sun would explode, disintegrating as a nova into oblivion. Conversely, without the great expanding masculine force, the staggering mass of a large sun would collapse upon itself into a black hole, and nothing would escape, not even light. The expanding and contracting forces depend on one another for balance.

The positive, expanding masculine potential has been absent in the lives of most delinquent boys. They are in desperate need of a man or men to contain them. Instead, they are often dependent on their mothers and cling to that solitary filial relationship. Without the containment and the blessing of older men, the adolescent boy goes out of control. The mothers of delinquent young men often find themselves in this all-too-common, no-win situation. They have been abandoned by their husbands and are raising their sons alone; yet they become the object of their sons' aggression and resentment. The boys grow physically bigger than their mothers, more powerful, faster. But they are still dependant, and they resent that their mothers are unable to meet their needs. The mothers can no longer chase their boys down. They can no longer discipline or restrain them. It is at that point that the delinquent boy will go out of control.

The most prevalent contributing factor to creating a delinquent boy is his missing father. Most delinquent boys are products of homes in which parental partnerships are out of balance.[41] The fathers have abandoned ship, and the mothers are often overwhelmed to the point of dysfunction.

Understanding Conduct Disorder

We must step out of the world of metaphor for a moment now and speak conventionally about conduct disorder. Before we can define what Conduct Disorder is, it is helpful to clarify common misperceptions about it. An adolescent is not diagnosed with Conduct Disorder because of smart-aleck remarks and some rule breaking. On the contrary, it is natural for children to rebel as they gradually unfetter themselves from parental control. This liberation happens in fits and starts. It is normal for teens to act out at times.

Additionally, the Diagnostic Statistical Manual warns that several clinical diagnoses are sometimes confused with Conduct Disorder. For example, Oppositional Defiant Disorder (ODD), like Conduct Disorder, includes disruptive behaviors: occasional loss of temper, defiance of rules, anger and spite, etc. ODD does not, however, include Conduct Disorder's aggression toward people or animals, destruction of property, theft, and deceit. Likewise, people who have Attention-Deficit/Hyperactivity Disorder (ADHD) also display some of Conduct Disorder's impulsive and disruptive behaviors. And the same goes for Adjustment Disorder.

Conduct Disorder is a clinical diagnosis made by a trained mental health professional using specific criteria. Conduct Disorder is described as a "[r]epetitive and persistent pattern of behavior in which the basic rights of others or major age-appropriate societal norms or rules are violated."[42] Conduct Disorder sufferers must also experience significant social, academic, or occupational disruption and are generally under the age of eighteen. They must have committed at least three heinous crimes (mugging, sexual assault, physical harm to persons or animals, etc.) within the last year and one such crime within the last six months.

Expressions of Conduct Disorder

Conduct Disordered individuals tend to have low empathy for others, if they have any sense of empathy at all, and most of them, if not all, have a zero-sum mentality. In other words, they perceive that their physical, emotional, and security needs will not be met unless they act aggressively to take from others. The result of this zero-sum mentality is a chronic state of self-centeredness. Because this mentality tends to originate during childhood, the behavioral pattern endures regardless of changing economic or social circumstances.

There is an old Jewish tale that will help make our point about conduct disorder's mindset. In heaven, the story goes, there is a massive cauldron of soup. It is made by the angels and saints with heavenly spices, vegetables, and broth. All the people in heaven sit around the soup, eager to eat. But God has played a trick and given everyone spoons with four-foot handles, making it impossible for any individual to feed him- or herself. The heavenly population finds a quick and natural solution, however. They scoop their long spoons into the nutritious broth, reach across the cauldron, and feed each other. No one goes hungry. Everyone gives and receives, feeding and being fed in return. There is a certain lightheartedness in this scene.

In hell, God has sent down another large cauldron of soup. It is every bit as nutritious and good-tasting as the heavenly soup, for the angels and saints have made this batch, too. And God has played the same trick with the spoons. Unlike the community-minded scene in heaven, however, no one reaches across to feed his or her neighbor. Everyone in hell goes hungry because no one shares. Everyone is only concerned with feeding him- or herself. Hell on earth is living in a family or a neighborhood where everyone is out for number one. Conduct Disorder, then, is essentially a vigilant and chronic state of deprivation brought on by persistent narcissism.

We tend to know who we are from the reactions of others. If our behavior offends one person, it might not be our problem. But if our behavior offends five people, then we had better take a look. The reason Conduct Disordered teens often get stuck in their self-centered ways is that they don't use the reactions of others as a way to gauge their own behavior, or, as a systems theorist might conclude, the cognitive feedback loops are broken. The reactions of others in the community simply don't motivate self-reflection.

Conduct Disorder sufferers tend to experience behavioral feedback as assault. Approach them with empathy, and they see insidious intent. Try to mentor them, and they smell a trap. Treatment feels like a hundred people yelling in a room, and the sound just hurts their ears.

Common core Conduct Disordered beliefs include:

I will never get what I need, so I have to take what I want.
The world is against me, so I have to be against the world.

The world is a dangerous place, so I have to be aggressive
  to protect myself.

Conduct Disordered individuals and socially healthy individuals have at least one thing in common: they violate the boundaries of others frequently. The difference is, of course, that socially healthy people create a buffer so the boundary violation is not repeated, they step back from the edge once they identify it. To the contrary, Conduct Disordered individuals find the edge and aspire to cross it. They love the power inherent in violating boundaries, breaking rules, and defying social norms. They get feedback from cops and the courts that their behavior is off, but they keep pushing and don't stop.

Adrian was a sixteen-year-old delinquent who had grown up on the streets. He had a history of stealing and getting into fights. One night the police nearly killed him. They were chasing him with dogs, and it looked like he wasn't going to get away. When cornered, he decided to crawl up on a garage roof. He pulled out a BB gun and stood on the top of the garage waving it around. The cops thought it was a high-caliber pistol and shot him in the neck, just missing his jugular vein. He fell to the ground, and he even cried. But his remorse was for getting shot, not for disrupting the neighborhood or frightening the police. Everything was about having a good time. The cops had made his fun by chasing him, but they ruined his fun by shooting him.

Teaching the Teachers

In "The Devil's Sooty Brother," the Dark Man simply appears in the forest when the lost boy needs him. He has no history that we know of, no childhood or any adolescence of his own. It is possible to come to the conclusion that men and women who channel Dark Man energy are simply born and grow to be mature and wise. Usually, the reverse is true.

The combination of maturity and wisdom required of community-minded adults is often spawned from initiatory processes or journeys similar to the one we are suggesting for delinquent boys. Those journeys often begin with confusion and often involve pain. The teacher's, the treatment professional's, or the mentor's journeys are often initiated by discomfort, disorientation, or some psychic, emotional, or spiritual wound. Some of the best agents of the Dark Man are those who have fallen and then got back up.

Wounds are not in and of themselves enough to pro-

duce emotional depth, however. The energy of the healing process must be channeled, and that channel must
involve other initiated individuals.

Channeling the Wound

Warren is an example of a mentor who channeled his
own wound into something productive. He is a thirty-
five-year-old businessman and father of two from Minneapolis. His wound came from an alcoholic father and
an angry, clingy mother.

"My father's contribution was violence and tyranny,"
Warren explained. "He was a bar fighter in his youthful
years, and he beat my mother several times. I remember waking up to holes in the living room wall from the
drunken brawls he'd have with his friends, and I remember a time when he had me cornered and threatened to
beat me because I vomited from the flu."

"So, you and your mother were the victims?" we asked.

"No. My mother was violent, too. I think she lived
out her aggression through him, and when they divorced
she was forced to own that. I remember when my father
was finally out of the house, she blew up at my brother
once and put his head through a window. She became
very angry at men and took it out on me and my broth-

ers, saying that men were responsible for all the evil on the planet, making fun of their body parts, and things like that."

"So, you had two angry parents?"

"Yes, but my mother compounded the damage, I think, with an enmeshed relationship with me. My dad was gone, so there was no balance. She always told me how beautiful and special I was and how I was different. But men were essentially evil. Well, I didn't have any choice; I was going to turn into a man someday. This put me in a terrible fix that took me years to work out."

"Can you give an example of how someone helped you channel your wound productively? A Dark Man?"

"Yes. When I was in my twenties I entered therapy. The therapist suggested I go to a men's conference. Many of the most productive spiritual and emotional experiences I have had have been at men's conferences. I remember once, the elders at a conference had the youngest participants gather in the middle of a field. I was twenty-six that year. I think the oldest man in the circle was in his early thirties. There were about ten of us.

"About ten older men formed a circle around us. None of the younger men knew what had been planned. Five other men had dressed up as demons and were hiding in the surrounding forest. They had masks and weapons. They looked pretty scary. They tried to attack the younger men in the center of the circle. The elder men fended the demons off."

"What was the effect?" we asked.

"Well, it was very dramatic. The men who played the demons were very convincing. Several of the protectors were actually injured. They had to really fight to force the demons away from the younger men."

"But how did it affect you personally?"

"I couldn't stop crying. It took a year or so to realize what had happened, but I eventually realized that my father had not been there to protect me. And it was a major contradiction to the message my mother had drummed into my head. There was something about men that was actually useful and good."

"What was the new message?"

"Now, after working with the issue for years, I would say that the message I have embraced is that when it comes to potential for good and evil, men and women really are equal. I no longer walk around as an apologist for my father or for other men. Just as no woman should be an apologist for their mothers or other women. I am an individual."

"Warren, you work with troubled kids. You have a successful marriage, and you seem to be doing a good job parenting your own children. How did that experience, that channeling of the wound, help you to become a community man?"

"I think if I hadn't been able to let go of the shame and blame, I would have been a passive-aggressive person. I've never been a violent or even an aggressive person, so I don't think I would have ever hurt anyone. But I wouldn't have been able to be present for anyone, either. I would have been too wrapped up in my shame."

Warren volunteers his time at a boys' correctional facility near where he lives.

The Unchanneled Wound

Agents of the Dark Man, if they are working with children or young adults, must be able to put their own egos or wounds aside at least enough to shoulder the projections of younger people. And in order to put your own wound aside, you must first own it and become conscious of its meaning.

Chuck was a psychotherapist who was unable to put his own issues aside. He worked in an adolescent correctional treatment program, the same one as Warren. He facilitated groups, monitored individual boys' progress, and performed some one-on-one sessions.

"You don't know what it's like to suffer," one of the incarcerated boys exclaimed. "You ain't never experienced something like what we do."

"Really," Chuck the psychotherapist replied. He sat up in his chair and took on a righteous tone. "Everyone has experienced pain. I had an abusive mother, who wasn't able to express her love for me. That was very painful in its own way. The way I acted out was to have many partners. I slept with many different women. That was my way of dealing with the pain. I used sex."

Several of the boys in the group shot glances back and forth.

"Chuck," one of the other staff interrupted. "Maybe we should move on. We've got time for one more group member to speak."

"Fine," said Chuck, "but it's important for everyone to know that everyone has experienced pain. I'm almost fifty years old, and I still struggle with my issues. I'm responsible for over one hundred kids, and it gets pretty overwhelming. I not only have to deal with my issues but I also have to deal with your issues, too."

Chuck justified his inappropriate tirade later, saying the boys would learn from his mistakes. But Chuck's unhealed wounds trumped his judgment and his professionalism. He brought his issues into the group and projected them onto one of his young clients. Essentially, Chuck was demanding emotional nurturing. He was unable to ask young men to go down and grieve because he had never done it himself.

Eventually, the stress of the job was too much and Chuck quit. Before he did, however, he had done significant damage. Instead of being an agent of the Dark Man, instead of blessing the boys by witnessing their processes and noting their wounds, he took from them. In his late forties he was still unformed and needy.

We imagine that Chuck was suspended in time. He was stuck at two or three years old, a stage of development when everything was about him. There may be many reasons for people like Chuck to be stuck. He may have been traumatized at some point. But it was likely that Chuck's needs were not satisfied as a child, and he became caught in that narcissism.

True agents of the Dark Man are the opposite of narcissistic. They have the ability, willingness, and drive to see the intrinsic value of every human being, regardless of how much destruction they have caused. Buddhists greet each other with their hands pressed together and say *namaste*, which implies "I see the god in you." Silently and metaphorically, that is the way agents of the Dark Man see delinquent boys.

Meeting the Princess

Alfred Adler noted:

> We may now understand that any rules that serve to
> secure the existence of humankind, such as legal codes,
> totem and taboo, superstition, or education, must be
> governed by the concept of the community and be
> appropriate to it. . . . We find adaptation to the commu-
> nity is the most important psychological function, both
> in the individual and in society. What we call justice and
> righteousness and consider most valuable in the human
> character is essentially nothing more than the fulfill-
> ment of the conditions that arise from the social needs
> of human kind.[43]

In "The Devil's Sooty Brother," we learn, after the fact,
that during his seven years tending the pots the young
corporal learned to play a musical instrument. John Turnipseed's music can be heard in his sermons, while Warren's might be heard in a session with a wounded boy.
The lost corporal, John Turnipseed, and Warren transformed wounds and hunger into something useful.

Once back on the surface of the earth, the king of
the earthly realm hears the corporal's music and loves it.

The boy is now able and willing to use his creative power to generate something beautiful. He feeds the very community that he would have likely destroyed had he not followed the direction of the Dark Man. His spine is no longer a bent rod. His mind, heart, and creative potential are aligned. He wears a smock, indicating that he has acquired humility and a willingness to accept delayed gratification, to focus on a goal or to labor for some greater good. The king recognizes his gifts and blesses him, as does the communal circle of adults (unions, guilds, associations, etc.). And it is a cyclical blessing. The young man's existence is now a blessing to the king and the community that blessed him.

Yet the story doesn't end there; if it did, we would be left hungry. If a man is a community man only, there will still be something missing in his life. To finish his story, the corporal, like most young men, must create a family of his own.

The King's Youngest Daughter

When an incarcerated boy begins to respond to therapy and many of his issues have been dealt with, he will inevitably turn some conversations toward the subject of romantic relationships. The advice that we often give (beyond respect and caring) comes from two lines paraphrased from Sam Keen's fine book about men, *Fire in the Belly*.[44] First, "Where are you going in your life?" And second, "Who will go with you?" Keen rightly emphasizes that these questions must be asked in this order, or a young man's ship may end up tossed about on turbulent seas.

Essentially, a young man's emphasis should be on what Joseph Campbell calls *bliss* or *passion*. Following your passion, we tell boys, will provide you with a direction and a theme. Women may come and go, but you will still have your passion. When you finally choose to marry, then you will have to establish a detente between your passion and the woman who has been elevated to the status of family. Until you find that special one, however, your passion or direction must dominate the script of your life. After you marry, keep your passion while fulfilling the requirements of being a husband and father. It is not one or the other. Rather, it is a balance between the two.

Being passionate about something makes a young man not only interested but also interesting. Choosing a woman should not be the object of his life, just as choosing a man should not be the object of a young woman's life. The object should be the creative goal, how one makes his or her mark on, or contributes to, the community and humanity.

In our story, the oldest daughter threatens to drown herself because our young man wears a smock. She does not recognize his gold (humility, integrity, focus, passion, creativity) as legitimately precious. Her revulsion is merely one more fruit borne of our hero's psychic and emotional labor. That such a woman is not attracted to him is actually a gift, and he has the Dark Man to thank for it. A Mercedes car or a Gucci handbag would have suited her better than a man with emotional and psychic depth. The youngest daughter, on the other hand, displays respect for the king; she values what can be beautiful in men. She treasures the very qualities that we as treatment professionals try to inspire in boys.

Eight

Conclusion

THE PROLIFERATION OF CRIMINAL GANGS IN THE EARLY nineties ushered in an unprecedented wave of adolescent crime. Almost every category of juvenile offense peaked around 1994. During that time, violent crimes committed by teens soared. Law enforcement, schools, and correctional treatment programs have managed to reverse the trend. The first decade of the twenty-first century has been less violent, but the numbers are still sobering. In 2008, law enforcement agencies in the United States arrested an estimated 2.11 million persons under the age of 18. Approximately 96,000 of those arrests were for violent crimes, such as murder (93 percent of which were committed by boys), forcible rape, robbery, and aggravated assault. About 40,000 arrests were for weapons possession. More than 439,000 arrests were for burglary, larceny-theft, stealing cars, and arson.[45]

According to an Iowa State University (ISU) study, the average murderer costs taxpayers approximately

$24 million. Each rape committed is estimated to cost $448,532, each armed robbery $335,733, each aggravated assault $145,379, and each burglary $41,288. These shocking figures led the head of the study, associate professor of sociology and director of the criminal justice program Matt DeLisi, to conclude: "[E]ven if a prevention program is very expensive—and most of them are actually shockingly inexpensive—they're still more cost effective than allowing these [criminal] careers to unfold."[46]

The power in young male bodies and minds must be channeled to protect and serve society rather than to tear it apart. The punishment model of corrections simply does not work. Yet millions enter the penal system as children and go on to bounce in and out of adult prisons.

In this book we have presented a metaphorical template for the process of working with troubled boys to turn them away from crime. The Brothers Grimm provided us with a very useful set of images for that purpose. Our presupposition is that every boy and young man should know in his heart that he is valued by the community at large, and especially by a community of men. He must know in his bones that his gifts are recognized and blessed.

Notes

1 Dante Alighieri. *The Portable Dante: The Divine Comedy*. New York: Penguin, 1977.

2 The Odysseus story was first used this way by Robert Bly at a men's conference in northern Minnesota, ca. 1988.

3 Von Eschenbach, Wolfram. *Parzival*, translated by A. T. Hatto. New York: Penguin, 1980.

4 Bly, Robert. *Iron John: A Book About Men*. New York: Addison Wesley, Inc. 1990.

5 This story has been compounded from several sources, Internet and oral, including: 4Literature. net, and Zipes, Jack. *The Complete Fairy Tales of the Brothers Grimm*. New York: Bantam, 1987.

6 "Pensacola New Pride: An Adlerian-based Alternative for Juvenile Delinquents." *Individual Psychology*, 1982, 38:129–37.

7 Campbell, Joseph. *The Power of Myth*. New York: Doubleday, 1988.

8 Rumi, Jalaluddin. *Delicious Laughter*, edited and translated by Coleman Barks. Athens, Ga.: Maypop, 1990. Reprinted with permission.

9   *The Mabinogion* translated by Lady Charlotte Guest, excerpted in *Bulfinch's Mythology: The Age of Fable, The Age of Chivalry, Legends of Charlemagne*, edited by Richard Martin. New York: Harper Collins, 1991.

10 Matthews, John, and Caitlin Matthews. *British and Irish Mythology: An Encyclopedia of Myth and Legend*. London: Diamond Books, 1995.

11 *Ibid.*

12 According to Wikipedia, the Hallstatt culture, which was dominant in central Europe between the eighth and sixth centuries BCE and spread from the Upper Rhine as far as the Danubian Lowland is linked with the Proto-Celtic and Celtic populations. See "Halstaff culture" and "Celts" on Wikipedia (accessed February 14, 2011).

13 Matthews and Matthews. *British and Irish Mythology, op. cit.*

14 Personal conversation with Robert Bly.

15 *Ibid.*

16 Rule, Warren R. "Lifestyle Self-Awareness and the Practitioner: Understanding and Reframing Resistance Using Angels and Devils as Metaphor." *The Journal of Individual Psychology*, 2000, 56:2:184–91.

17 Maley, Michael J. *Living in the Question: An Explo-*

ration of Formlessness, Change, and Healing. Minneapolis, Minn.: Bodysmart, 1995.

18 Campbell, Joseph. *Creative Mythology.* New York: Penguin, 1968, p. 35. Quoted in Joseph Campbell, *The Mythic Dimension: Selected Essays 1959–1987.* Novato, Calif.: New World Library, 1997.

19 Online Etymology Dictionary <www.etymonline.com/index.php?term=epiphany> (accessed February 14, 2011).

20 Bly. *Iron John, op. cit.*

21 Washington State Institute for Public Policy, (2006), *Evidence-Based Public Policy Options to Reduce Future Prison Construction, Criminal Justice Costs, and Crime Rates,* Olympia, Wash.

22 Lawrence, D. H. "Fantasia of the Unconscious" in *Psychoanalysis and the Unconscious and Fantasia of the Unconscious.* New York: Penguin, 1988.

23 *Ibid.*

24 Bly, Robert, personal conversation.

25 Moore, Robert from a Minnesota men's conference, ca. 1980s.

26 Bly, Robert, personal conversation.

27 Meade, Michael, from a men's conference, ca. 1980s.

28 Meade, Michael. *Men and the Water of Life: Initia-*

tion and the Tempering of Men. New York: Harper Collins, 1993.

29 Walsh, David. *Why Do They Act That Way?: A Survival Guide to the Adolescent Brain for You and Your Teen*. New York: Free Press, 2004.

30 Siegel, Daniel J. *The Developing Mind: How Relationships and the Brain Interact to Shape Who We Are*. New York: Guilford, 1999.

31 Ansbacher, Heinz L., and Rowena R. Ansbacher. *The Individual Psychology of Alfred Adler: A Systematic Presentation in Selections from His Writings*. New York: Basic, 1956.

32 Siegel, *The Developing Mind, op. cit.*

33 *Ibid.*, p. 18.

34 Walsh. *Why Do They Act That Way? op. cit.*

35 *Ibid.*

36 See David H. Olson, Ph.D. and Blaine J. Fowers in *Family Therapy: An Overview* (6th Edition), edited by Irene and Herbert Goldenberg. Pacific Grove, Calif.: Brooks/Cole, 2004.

37 This experiential family systems concept was articulated by Carl Whitaker (1912–1995).

38 *Ibid.*

39 This is a structural family systems concept articulated by Salvador Minuchin (1921–).

40 This is a strategic family systems concept articulated by Jay Douglas Haley (1923–2007).

41 Executive function is a strategic family systems concept also articulated by Haley.

42 Diagnostic and Statistical Manual of Mental Disorders. Washington, D.C.: American Psychiatric Association, 2006.

43 Adler, Alfred. *Understanding Human Nature*. Center City, Minn.: Hazelton, 1998.

44 Keen, Sam. *Fire in the Belly*. New York: Bantam, 1991.

45 Puzzanchera, Charles. *Juvenile Arrests 2008*, the Office of Juvenile Justice and Delinquency Prevention Juvenile Justice Bulletin: U.S. Department of Justice, 2009.

46 DeLisi, Matt, *et. al.*, *ISU Team Calculates Societal Costs of Five Major Crimes; Finds Murder at $17.25 Million*, Iowa State University News Service, September 27, 2010.